I0623351

LAST BACCHANALE

NEW POEMS BY GEORGE WALLACE

ROADSIDE PRESS

Cover Concept: Candil Vandil
Cover Art: Nicolas Poussin's painting *Bacchanal in Front of a Statue of Pan*

Editor: Michele McDannold

Roadside Press
Colchester, IL

TABLE OF CONTENTS

Next came Dionysus, the son of the virgin,
bringing the counterpart to bread: wine
and the blessings of life's flowing juices.
His blood, the blood of the grape,
lightens the burden of our mortal misery
  —Euripides, The Bacchae

HIRED MEN

When I bend my ear to the feral land I hear them all, hired
men, shotguns roaring, battles raging among them, soil, bone,
wheels and locomotives, sparks flying, enormous and untamed
and ready to turn on each other at the drop of a hat; scouts,
cooks, cavalry boys, blind charges and tin trumpets blaring,
nations pursuing nations, guard dogs straining to the limit of
their chains, and all the lonely young men writing letters home;

when I bend my ear and hear their enchantments and disap-
pointments, chasing sirens of some lesser god, unattainable
glory or only the narrow glittering eye of the horizon, I hear
them all; woodlands parting, campfires blazing, unkind witness
and daredevils dared, wine spilled like blood, brushfires pillag-
ing halfway through Montana; grasslands bending with wind;
from here to California, not soothed by the wind, but fed by it;
not seduced by the sun, but accustomed to its double-crosses;

broke-tooth and unbeaten, trail dust from ear to ear, eyes
like mud, hearts like ruts of wagon wheels, I hear them all,
boastful; the hired men, rough coats and plain, skip jacks and
blacksmiths, spike maul hammerboys; willing to sleep in grav-
el and snow if it will keep them out of jail, the bully and the
outcast lying side by side; the mamma's boy willing to pound
a thousand miles of rail if it will prove something to his mates;
card sharps and horse thieves, grub not worth eating being
thrown into the fire;

unreasonable men taming an unreasonable land, pissing in the
illimitable bushes; and bosses whose voices grate in their ear
like thunder;

hired men, their bones left out in the open air to dry, compan-
ion to buffalo, extinct now, for all practical purposes, like the
million miles of hooves which preceded them.

IT IS POSSIBLE TO LOVE

It is possible to love, if you ignore the blackness at the heart of the red red rose; or the loyalty of bees suffocating in honey-combs; the wetness of tears shed artificially, or doubt burrowing like a trench digging road machine through selflessness and servitude;

it is possible to love, if you ignore the paper dragons and irksome smiles, the insect nesting in pretty petals, the inauspicious highway; the pessimism of roots dug way too deep into the poor soil of unreality; and the concrete facts and raw intangibles;

and the poisonous gas of green envy raging in the well, and the unresolved kisses and unrestrained desire; and the unexplained impulsiveness of youth and beauty squandered, and murderous lobotomy of mistrust passed freely through rooms and eye to eye;

it is possible to love, it is possible to love, and necessary; though the world's gone mad or been gutted at the butcher block; though logic and good sense race away at the speed of light, though a hollow echo sounds in the empty heart like a corpse bell;

and the rot spreads fast through floorboards and kitchen walls; and the vanishing point comes on faster than a fist through a fun-house mirror;

to love, to love, and ignore the galaxies crumbling around us and the cold empty vastness of space that reaches into every heart; though memento mori and other ethical reminders and imperatives escape us, and the compost heap that piles up and festers and consumes the horizon also consumes us;

though fruitflies prosper in the appleflesh of days;

though the north wind blows and blows; and the unrepentant viciousness of the world claws at our nightmare windows, and opens up all the right doors in all the wrong ways.

HARD TO IMAGINE

It is hard to imagine certain things, like a good book on a summer day, like time going slow, like peaches growing on apple trees; or old habits that lie dormant as ghosts for twenty years, but never go away; hard to imagine, hard to imagine, how to turn back the tide, how to overcome fear, or ignore the salt taste of tears in a movie theatre;

like the return of forsythia blossoms in spring; like the inconstancy of gods; like a young man dreaming on a Sunday afternoon in March after he has first fallen in love; hard to imagine; hard to imagine, like an old clock on a mantel that sets itself ticking; like an argument avoided in a small cafe, like baby turtles escaping a viper's nest and crawling away; like the love between a woman and a man surviving under a microscope;

hard to imagine; hard to imagine, but necessary, every last one of them, and harder to picture, though if you close your eyes and listen carefully you can hear them, they give themselves away; like a stolen umbrella opening and closing in a hallway closet; like sunlight pouring back into the sky, horizon to horizon after winter rain;

like the sweet original melody of stars pulsing tender in the night after an absence of ten thousand years.

I LIVE INSIDE A CHALK-DRAWN CIRCLE

I live inside a chalk-drawn circle, the line I draw around my-
self; I am the monkey wrench, the fly in the ointment, conduc-
tor of a trolley that never knew a track, a chemist concocting
illegal rhymes, I hand out citations to anybody, I teach the
snow to fall, the stones beneath the surface of the green green
sea to sing, I cast out evil when evil shows its face;

I live inside a chalk-drawn circle, I am incurious of sinners,
indifferent to soldiers, a magickal thinker who wanders among
the ruins wearing bedroom slippers and taking notes, a child
at the most serious play, dangerous and free; I live inside the
chalk circle and tell tales concerning societies and men, a
canary that never knew a cage, baker of a kind of bread that
never felt a knife; I am a maker of roof tiles that never felt the
falling rain;

and I sing my song and whole gardens appear where the
bombs once fell, I herd giraffe on tenement rooftops, I wave my
hand and paintings appear on hospital walls; I am the secret
mixologist of dreams, I live in a pottery jar and wait to be filled,
I live in a glass pitcher and wait to be emptied, left alone in my
prison I take my time and study the darkness;

an earthquake that never made a table shake, a crust of bread
that never swept itself under the carpet; I live inside a chalk-
drawn circle, a lie never told, a love never betrayed, a vice that
never happened; a lighter of imaginary dynamite;

and I puncture fear and outlaw love; and outlast anything
which lives outside the chalk-drawn circle.

YOU MUST BE THIS CRAZY

You must be this crazy, you must be this brave, you must be
this tall, in spirit and in pluck, to climb this wall, to ride this
ride, to do this dance, to see beyond danger, to face taunts &
abuse and want to come here in the first place;

you must be this strong, you must be this bold, you must be
this stupid, to outwit coyotes, mules, uniformed and redneck
vigilantes with their jeeps & helicopters and their freedom to
hate;

with their drones & dogs & infra-red plutocratic ugly cowboy
attitudes;

you must be this blind to see past the trouble & disrespect in
the eyes of your fellow man; in the eyes of the pious, in the
eyes of the fearful, in the eyes of the rich & well-fed;

you must eat your pride & swallow your honor; you must keep
your fists in your pockets & your prick in your prison mattress;
you must be this hungry, you must be this chaste, you must
be this despairing, this humble;

to give up your homeland, to give up your name, to give up
your family, to say goodbye to the people you love, to strap all
you possess onto your honest back in a great big gunny sack

and wade like the snakebit through fog & mist, through river &
eternity, through desert & mud

to the fat chance gringo promised land

ONCE I WAS A TURKISH BOY

Once I was a Turkish boy educated at the breast of an olive
tree; once I was a Kurdish freedom fighter on a mountain track
(I have dodged helicopters since I was ten, and spiked Russian
tanks like a child in spring, spearing snakes in a frogpond)

Once I was the son of a Greek
    in broad pants singing
Bing
       Bang
Boom
whilst walloping cookpots in Cleveland Ohio

Once I was the daughter of an Egyptian general with stars on
his epaulets, I wore bangles & a Rolex; my lips were hazel my
complexion blue; I was smooth as lapis lazuli in a jewel-stud-
ded crown of scorn.

THE CENTER IS EVERYWHERE

The center is everywhere, nowadays I go tender as a shudder-
ing angel when resilience is called for, other times I am hard as
a candyapple and legal as fuck, slow to react to life's stimula-
tions but most of the time I take life like I take my women (like
a lump of sugar in the cheek) because life's a bitch life's okay
so what if something happened one hot day in August 1968
while the suckers were on their knees begging for it;

the center cannot hold the center dissolves in a man's throat
the center doesn't give two shits about you or me; one day I
was walking thru Tompkins Square I had a hardhat on and
this vision came to me, William Blake in a Humvee; I kept my
head I never told nobody what I saw;

another time I was pressing elevator buttons in the lobby of
the Chelsea hotel with Leonard Cohen laughing out loud with
Jean-Michel Basquiat;

O how swell the whole mess and movement of the city seems
to me, swirling around the two of us like a mocha latte barber
pole! buses bats steam shovels subway trains!

O! let us ride high as far and fast as fast,
farther than far, far away!

AN OPEN AND SHUT CASE

An old man who used to untie his little skiff in the harbor and go out to sea (leaving his room before dawn) no longer leaves his room before dawn to set sail;

he sits by a window in a straight back chair, with his pipe and his glasses and his golden retriever, like a pitcher on a table with water in it, but no flowers;

he sits and waits for the sea, which used to pull at his blood, to fill him up; waits for the sea, calls on the sea, asks the sea to say his name, with its salty tongue of brine and coffers of fish;

an old man sits by a window
    and looks out at the sea;
    and the sea sits by a window
and looks in on an old man;

an old man with eyes that open and shut like a mill pond race with a one way gate to catch the tide; an old sea, with an old manner of catching and releasing men;

the tide comes in, the tide goes out, you catch the tide, it is as simple as that;

an old man who no longer sets sail sits by a window, looks out at a sea he no longer understands, and opens and shuts his eyes;

shuts his eyes and opens them, like the wings of a butterfly that has perched on a harbor rock too long; he has missed the great migration home.

A SMALL CHILD IN THE SACRIFICIAL SHADOWS

A small child looks out through poplars and snowy pines at
a fivepoint buck crossing the winter field, in the distance is a
black mountain that bars the way north; he is like a village
woman looking for gossip to believe in; there isn't a malicious
bone in his body; no enchantment yet either, though the sight
of a deer brings him joy, makes him feel a little richer for the
experience;

in the distance, beyond the fields, a cloud lingers over the
black mountaintop, wreathed in rocks; wind blows free as bird
song, blowing snow;

a small child listens to the wind, wanders where the poplars
shriek and the low pine branches moan; the world is taxed
with snow, but he does not know about taxation yet, or met-
aphor, or the ways of men, he does not know the heavy load
most men must bear;

a small child is helpful when the village men make crosses,
helpful when the village women beat hay with the branches of
fallen trees; a small child is helpful when his father cuts wood
in autumn, and is careful not to be a distraction, that's how
accidents happen;

one day there is an argument in the village over money or
pride, and a small child's father is killed;

now the small child is a young man who shaves by a clear
stream, a young man dressed like his father, he has ice blue
eyes, his father wore rags, so he does too; his father laid out
shingles tight and even, now he does the same, he does this for
his poor old widowed mother; a young man is his father al-
ready, though he does not yet know it;

now he is a young man standing at the apron of the black
mountain with an axe in his hand; it is spring, fat sheep are
watering by a clear mountain stream, some children are sing-
ing a religious song, no sign of the fivepoint deer anywhere;

a young woman passes, her eyes linger on the young man's
torso too long, and probe his eyes; the young man looks this

way and that; he is shy of girls, he keeps his eyes trained on the monotony of his work, or on the roadway which leads from the village all the way to the capital city;

he is so shy the young man goes away on the black mountain road, and it is several years before he returns; he has been with working men in the city, he has drunk hard in taverns; he returns with some coins in his head, no wiser to the world despite all his work in soldiering or prison or wisdom-gathering; he is the same young man as before, though he wears a beard and his shoulders are broader and more square;

now he takes the young woman by the hand, he places her hand into the open breast of his shirt, not just for the warmth; her small hands are little fists of aromatic herbs, her lips are pomegranate; her breath is perfume and potion; he does not understand this thing but cannot do without it;

the young woman and the young man wander in the tall grass where the fivepoint buck used to stand; they make love on a green grassy hill; the young man takes his sweetheart in his arms and they do a wedding dance;

now they are married, they plunge laughing into a cottage bed; his arms to her are like a chapel door made of good wood, her arms to him are a waltz through the magic woods with sunlight splashing; their laughter is a knife plunged deep into ice-cold rushing water;

things do not go well—the marriage is barren, or a child falls in a well; perhaps there are river floods, or else a madman with some supernatural power and time on his hands who comes along and steals his wife away;

overnight his life is over, his arms are tired, his confidence crushed; overnight the customary rituals no longer hold power; winter returns, crops wither in the field or rot on the vine; his life is reduced, he is a lesson to the others, no we must not be like him! the village men sneer, the village women have endless things to say about the matter;

first it was his legs, then his heart; then he was silent and blind in his armchair, blind as the black stone mountain;

all across the village, it is snowing again; the kitchen fire flickers, shadow of dying flames cross themselves on the cottage wall, like so many tiny priests in the vestry; the old man is dying in long silhouette, by firelight, with no one in the room to tell his story to;

an old man is a looking glass plate of all his days, just an old man; trapped like a moth in a cottage room, anyone may look in and sooth him or watch him die, but they seldom do;

one day the fivepoint deer returns, stands outside the old man's cottage, who can explain this visitation; that day, the old man dies, dies in his own bed, cold as stone, alone in the sacrificial shadows;

at the moment the old man's soul escapes his body a small boy peers in through the old glass panes of his cottage window, with wonder and just a little joy in his heart; it is as if the old man is some kind of black mountain to him, it is as if the old man is some kind of fivepoint deer.

THE OBJECT OF MY DESIRE

Because life was so much younger and full of surprises back
in the tenderloin years and the girl from my bible school was
all grown up and stood six foot tall to a Colorado mountaintop
and was soft and reasonable, smooth as the Bossa Nova and
magnificent as a cloud, and wore a pink parka when she came
back home from college;

because it was snowing out and I heard her telling beautiful
lies, and everybody who didn't go to college expected to get
drafted and I figured before I got shot in Vietnam I'd let sex
drugs and rock and roll do their beautiful thing;

because it was the era of liberation and I was grasping like a
drowning man for a lifeline to freedom, and I thought I needed
to stick it to the man before the man stuck it to me;

I took the old pike road to Boston, to see her, in my father's
pea-green Oldsmobile, parked the car near the Combat Zone,
and walked through the dogshit and icy rain through a turn-
stile and found my way to the back of the bar where she told
me she was working;

I stood there in the dark shaking like a nervous puppy that
had been leashed too long to a parking/ meter and somehow
slipped its collar and didn't know what to do about it;

and I watched her work her stuff on stage for the crowd, feeling
dirty ashamed and blue;

feeling neglected and stupid, her not even knowing I was there,

my fist in my pocket, tight as an unripe plum, ready to fight
any man who stood between me and the object of my desire

TERRA FIRMA

Terra Firma, nest of days
with your golden planetary manners,
it would not do to possess you,
or the idea of you, or your raw eager magic,
it would not do to disturb your hue,
alter or explain the singularity
of your being, your chemistry,
or the curious nature, more strange
than good, by which you were born;
you are a collision of star bodies,
a terrestrial handshake, you're
a celestial outrage, too precious,
too powerful, too ecstatic for the stoic mind;
too rare for alchemy or meddling;

the last thing I would do is repackage you in my own image;

it would not do,
to meet you in human terms
or spell you out in 19th century
rhyming couplets, when your broad hips
hold tectonic sway; make use of you,
churn you for butter;
restrain or refashion or dam you up,
rescue you from yourself; no!
rather to deep dive into your bottomless,
terrapin pool of elegiac forgetfulness;
rather to be some gone western star,
eclipsed, robbed of the quintessential,

    than be your plunderer; rather
be fabric to your steel, rather
    be Noah to your great deluge,
servant to your limbs and legs
    and your magnificent arching rainbow neck;

rather be rendered insensible before you—
you big blue beautiful
starship you.

FEVER PITCH

An artist is born when the gatekeeper of straddling realities
looks the other way; thus it was, and it ever shall be; your body
is a transmitter for the gods; especially in the dark when we
are in our Max Ernst moment, when we are at fever pitch;

thus it was, the day the elderly gentleman dressed as a prim-
itive woodland fiend (with elkhorns on his head and eyes like
poppyseeds) walked into the room and threw a big damn party
for the little man;

we knew it was all over then; one knows what one knows and
keeps good counsel;

meanwhile, outside the room, servants wandered to and fro,
bearing secrets like canapés on silver trays;

father, possessing the appetite and grip of a mountain cat,
threw himself on the victuals, nearly ate them all; mother, with
her feet propped on an ottoman in another room, smoked a
hookah and dreamed her dream;

artists know how this thing goes, and how it must work; cry
and you cry alone; laugh and the music will playon and play
on; and all across the universe molecules known and unknown
will vibrate like cellphones ringing off the hook;

the little man clapped his hands, and the woodland creatures
danced! danced off the monstrous wallpaper; danced and
danced into the world; and a zebra and a unicorn threw them-
selves into a mad embrace!

and rattlesnakes rattled to see such sport, they crowded the
room, they rattled til their rattles fell off;

and in the miracle of blood and random feathers, another artist
was born.

PUNK ANGEL DIAMOND TATTOO

Punk angel diamond tattoo crowbar in a leatherjacket
jade frog in a shallow pond
    swamp Buddha in the hall of nations
you are my mirror you got a long gone tongue
your ashtray eyes your scent of wildflower
your sunlight on a window sill

    you are dangerous to me
and drive me wild

Punk angel carbon blue inheritance
swollen river in post-industrial gloom
    what flows, flows
your blood your schemes
your furious brains spilled out in sidewalk dawn
your chemical knowledge and hideous is as hideous does

    I am low-rise too
I am your diamond tattoo

      no apology
    no paint job
no you

ASSASSINATION

Ten ccs and a needle will kill a man as easy as a dumptruck
full of manure, or a shot of anti-freeze, or a little push off a
high balcony; all we need for this job is a noose or a knife, a
neck to slice, a voice to silence;

we are an unhappy people in an unknown territory, we might
have avoided this had we paid attention and taken steps earli-
er, if we had known the smell of carnations for what it signifies,
if we had known what it means to be men who will **no** longer
fight for their own freedom, but fight to take freedom away
from others;

we who have watched the mouths of the oligarchs open wide
and swallow us
we who have allowed the confidence of stooges to grow and
grow
we who become blinded by sly asides and obvious aggressions
and gloating cruelty and slick subversions
and open lies and sneering rallies;

we who have seen our dreams explode like stars in the blue
rotted sky of revolution;

salute you!

JUNKIE FERRARI

I
So much depends
upon

a pediatrician in a red
Ford

parked
by a fencepost

sporting
a white straw hat.

II
the prisoners of
            god
        churn on earth
like butter, until
    there is nothing left
  to turn

III
too
young
to be

so
dead

    Daddy

A BEING, ONLY A BEING

a Kansas City poet returns to the Ozarks
I rise repeatedly, in the gifted fist of time, a being, only a be-
ing, strong of bone, thick as a number two pencil, I rise, renewed
surfaces over old, give myself over to water, infinite, unguided, my
life like Rilke, my time lived in widening circles;

so these are the arms of earth;

weightless, a being, no more gripped in the vice of experience, one
part chinquapin, one part river rat, newly leafed, rooted in the
deep soil of rivers, barefoot, proud of every earth
worm that hammers the groove, digs the loam,

the small logic and great adventure;

being, only being, swimming with sunfish, bumping noses with
river rock and spawn;

the wren mimics me, and i am caught in the hair of eternity,
lonesome as the turquoise heart of mountain chains Ozark cast-
away, a fine being, only a being in a still pool horizon, rising to
the surface

a chipmunks gave my tongue first utterance,

yes I am deepwelling
yes, I am made mystic
yes, I am restored
          after Jeanette Powers

LUCK PLAYS A PAPAGO FLUTE

In a dusty little plaza in a
Sonoran town that everybody
knows but hasn't been
invented yet luck is a folk
singer carrying a tune most
people have forgot; luck
strings his guitar both ways,
he plays a Papago Flute;

luck is a beautiful man,
though nobody knows it;
with a voice like woven
palm leaves, which he
inherited from his father;
with a voice like a rope
and a heart like an
old empty bucket;

luck recognizes the face
staring back at him from
the bottom of the well;

just another folk singer
between Nogales and
Hermosillo, a little
unsettled, a little sad,
a little unstrung, though
he hides that carefully;
luck hides the wildness,
being his father's son;

luck walks past orphans,
thieves and walnut trees
in and out of sunlight, in
and out of the dark little bars,
spitting twice into the darkness for luck

HEART OF PINE, PETALS OF A ROSE

Day believes in night, night in day, and the earthworm believes
in the wet darkness which surrounds us all—corpse, genius,
infant in the womb;

the stopwatch at the end of the track believes in the athlete's
luminous stride; the stoplight at the end of the street believes
in its power to halt men in their ceaseless going; and the miser
believes in the copper pennies they place on his two dead eyes;

love believes in love, hate hates; the young believe in a revolu-
tion that can stop, for all time, the evil human reckoning;

the captor believes in the power of prison bars and shackles
and fear to hold men down; and the captive, languishing in the
belly of his cell, rubs his eyes in disbelief, believes in nothing,
only horses, horsewhips, and dreams of liberty;

fall believes in spring, and summer fall; night believes in day,
daylight in the wet darkness which surrounds us; and the
earthworm eats through everything, equally; root, stem, heart
of pine, petals of the rose;

and the young girl, who rises late in spring and trips merri-
ly to church in her sunday best, and believes in the sound of
church bells ringing.

SEVEN THOUSAND YEARS OF CO-EXISTENCE

Between the olive grove and the olive branch, the hardened fist of man; between the olive grove in the east and the olive grove in the south, war;

which nation rises against which nation? where are the intervening eyes of a truly benificent god?

between the ministrations of an all-knowing god and the ministrations of a war-like god, diplomats;

between the desert sun and the arms of a woman who rocks her baby to sleep at night, menace;

the song of a warbler singing in an olive tree is short, but sweet; sweet as the life span of an olive flower in an infant's hand;

to sleep well at night and dream of olive groves in full blossom, there's the trick, it is the most sublime benefaction of man;

when will mankind know eternity?

a nation that wages peace with its neighbor shall harvest its fields and fatten its stock in great abundance;

when will the child come who declares peace eternal among?

until then, war upon war, even if separated by seven thousand years of co-existence.

SHEVCHENKO'S SONG

*"We had just begun to break the chains that bind our folk in
slavery"—Taras Shevchenko*

And spring will return, placed on an altar like the golden fleece,
like snowclouds on the grievous horizon, and with it the sea;
Spring will return, rising, and with it Medea, returning to Col-
chis, and with it Jason to Thessaly; like the armies of the east
rising, like curses rising from the throats of thugs and maraud-
ers from the north; rising, rising, from the cloud and hoof of
steppe warriors on mounted horses;

and the eyes of the brotherhood shall be watchful; and Taras,
my Kobzar brother, will sing, plucking blind as tears at the
bandura, songs of war, of peace, of love and death and victory
and regret; how all men's ambitions turn to dust, how like ash-
es the taste of freedom dies in men's mouths;

Taras, my brother, will sing!
songs written with the entrails of the sun,
    songs written in long silver script of cloud,
songs written in blood, because hearts take root
where hearts have bled;

and we shall be fox among the foxes; and in the arms of hun-
ger rise with the wounded, and sing Shevchenko's song; and I
shall hold you again, and caress your yellow hair, longbraided
in the sun, and sing away your suffering, and tell the secrets of
your mouth, the cavernous depths of your soul;

hearts take flight; and the soul of a people cannot be replaced
or removed; and there is no literature greater than the song of
the Kobzar; and there is no literature more true than the song
of a people after their granaries have been plundered, their
harvest put to the torch;

and a small child is trembling in the tall grass, and peace is as
small as a speck of grain in a rabbit's eye.

PLAIN AS A WHISTLE WHEN THE CLOCK RUNS OUT

Girls like butterflies repopulate the city in spring why even
in late November when the dead leaves blow you may catch a
glimpse of one of them jogging westward w/ a friend

or catching a cab on 2nd Avenue for greener pastures uptown
or maybe Meadowlands New Jersey where the football fans w/
money in their pockets & time on their hands go

why just the other day in the bar of unrealizable dreams on
a wind crossed Sunday afternoon with the game on the big
screen (can't remember was it the Giants Jets or New Orleans
Saints)

a young girl walked in (she had hips like buttercups & eyes like
Montauk Daisies) & the sad young faces brightened & for one
sweet moment in the flickering death of blue artificial light

& it stopped raining penalty flags in everybody's head all the
false hopes unreal expectations all the knee-jerk accusations &
timeclock miseries we endure in our lives declared themselves
null and void, slipped out of the room & back into the world

yes it all came clear to me then so perfect so obvious so simple
& so true

Plain as first & ten
Plain as fourth & goal
Plain as a whistle when the clock runs out

the purposeless grace of God's sweet bottom line

ACCIDENTAL HOEDOWN

At the dark end of the street where the streetlight flickers and thunder lies in wait like a black cat with murder on its mind and night gives away its feline propositions with a flick of the nervous tail and the east river flows, it flows, easy as a beat cop on patrol—slip it into gear, rat catcher!

the Empire State is sure of its lies, citizenship is capitulation and there are hi-tech new ways of rounding up anyone who resists, they don't need no stinking draft and there's no safe place to go, the worst is about to do its best to fuck us up again;

and I'm not certain of much but I'm certain there's no way home, the situation and the traffic and the stream of night is unsteady and I am a shambles of a man, pregnant with confessions compromises and terrible purple prose;

I am the spray paint angel the graffiti boy, zipping, unzipping, zipping my leather jacket, nervous in the spotlight, hoping for a temporary answer to a permanent question (America has intentions nobody I know understands) and I am a crowbar I am a demon on the open mic I am a last resort;

and I'm in a broke down breaking/entering last ditch state of mind and I'm 17-years old again, jack-knifing across the FDR a half man in no-man's land, land of the estuarine, plenty to bend myself around to get this weary body to sanctuary;

North America is my home, c-section nation, dark as blood to a river I take my dive I dance my accidental hoedown dance, drunk on disobedience with lobotomized eyes;

I have got a mischievous foul-pole for a friend

STEADY AS A BUFFALO IN THE MOTOR OIL AISLE

It was not my first time at the rodeo, but it was my first time
hauling my ass back east from California, and I needed a drink
and a place to piss and rest my head; I was in a truck stop
somewhere in North Dakota, examining a display of red ban-
danas and I was killing time;

and I saw her, steady as a buffalo in the motor oil aisle, leaning
against a stack of Valvoline cleaning the mud and snow cake
out of her boots with a snow scraper she had lifted off a rack;

the East and West of her, her lateral clarity, calm as a dog that
don't scratch, with an interior kind of honesty, indifferent to
the swirl of joysticks and candy bars and anti-theft electronic
devices all around her;

she was a box-elder on a prairie promontory, a bad red road
sign pointing nowhere, her neck tattoos were immaculate and
her arms like inlaid pearl;

no ghost of a creature you might read about in a dime store
novel or meet someplace in Sacramento or was haunted by, no,
she was fierce, she was determined, she was full blooded and
no bullshit, experienced in practices I barely knew existed;

she knew 13 ways to shoot her way out of North Dakota, none
of them legal, and she had traveled all of them;

high strung, completely in control, a Gibson Guitar slung over
her back; hitching up her honest workman's jeans in a dishon-
est world and wearing the kind of sunglasses you might take to
a pistol range;

how the sunrise broke in both her eyes, like an optical illusion
and eclipsed mine! how calmly she carried a Dolly Parton CD
around in her left hand, waiting for the split second when the
clerk wasn't watching to pocket it;

I stood there like a fool in a truckstop in North Dakota in
spring, dazzled by her, and I let her go.

WHEN WE HAD A HEART

Once when like a big fire truck blowing thru rush hour traffic to rescue the world from itself, and our free souls began their journey through the world, not with it or against it, just through it; and love was the word and hearts were near to bursting on every doorstep and in every puddle and plate;

once when in the reflection of possibilities, like a belly full of miracles pure hearts brewed to overfilling despite the cold realities, and grew round and red as radishes; and we had had enough of all the bullshit that surrounded our all too human existences and were ready to change the world;

and once when, shimmering over the city like fm radio, a new kind of music sucked all the bad air out of our miserable and deranged animal brains and replaced it with collective joy, and ignorance and prejudice were defrocked and sent off to the ashpits of history to contemplate their many crimes; and the world put on its new suit of clothes and surprised itself in the mirror with how good it looked again, and went out into society and overcame its own imperfect nature and smiled;

life was fire, something you could almost taste, in the genuine equine motion of our bodies approaching each other openly on a dance floor you could smell the smouldering ecstasy;

you could just feel it; nobody was gonna bring us down again no not this time;

and the music sparked, and the streets were to us like the trajectory of stars; and love sweetened our tongues for each other, like spiced rum; and you extended your hand to mine and I took it, and offered mine the same;

and the dayglo laughter of every woman and man sang a panegyric to every other man woman and child, and we were momentarily free;

free, and no small brain politicians to fuck us up; free, and no perp walk or betrayal or anger or hate of manufactured war to shame us; free, until our lungs hurt to bursting with so many kindnesses, like too much cotton candy at the fair;

and we hung around on the edge of a cliff on a western shore
and waited for the sun to go down; and we were magnified,
magnified, and never made to feel small.

when we had a heart, that is
    not like today
when we had a very big heart

LOOK THRU ANY WINDOW

I see children of the field in their white working blouses who sing in wheat and carry socialist machetes into capitalist sugarcane or cellphones to the anarchist barricades and ignore the inconsistencies;

I sing like crickets in trees and study the textbook of the stars and they would die if they had to **sing** their song sing alone;

I see tenement children in slacks and blue jersies who sing in milk and run down applecart stairs and capture the flag and make a racket inside chimneypots and occupy tuberculosis wards and piss in hotel parking garages;

and children of the outcast for whom shaking down the man is an act of god, and life is **a** gumball machine and defiance is not a crime, and they would die if they could not be defiant;

I see children of the boulevard and children of gypsies and seafaring men who sing on Gulf Coast shores and collect like driftwood in the mouths of rivers; and share tattoos and build bonfires that touch the moon and never look back;

children of Greenwood Mississippi who sing in cotton and throw seductive eyes at each other all summer behind the general store, and gather kindling wood by the fork road when winter sets in;

and they slice up the night like a river of gold, and they are the night;

here's to them all, I would sing with them!

Navajo children, Nahuatl children, children of the corn, postage stamp children, children after a long drive home; children in the bleachers and swallowed up whole by the factory whistle;

Ethiopian children, London children, children of Nicaragua and Faeroe islands and Meso-American children in the fog;

children of the grandee and the satrap, children of the holy sativa and refugee camp;

children of the fast uproarious Asian plateau;

children of the souk the savannah and the heavenly oceanic surf, clothed in innocence and opportunity;

I would sing with them all! through masque of death and on every bombed out plain; children of children, folksingers hand-clappers dancers and players of the grass harp; in their hand me down shoes, or wearing no shoes at all; in rice fields and golden temples, on football pitches and in the delicate gardens of Versailles, dancing cumbia on tarmacs and runaway trains, conspiratorial in the redwoods, negotiating the dubious heights of Inwood, New York, doing pushups with Jim Carroll for a drug;

and in gloomy European shadows, carrying black and white Bibles;

and in the textbooks and holy books, fulfilling their father's promises to Science or God;

children holed up in laboratories and philosophical towers and academic halls, cooking up principles and certainties and devotions that will surely rescue every suffering thing in this world from itself, including themselves;

children and children and children again, who sing in milk, who sing in agriculture, who sing in wheat;

I would sing with them all, I would die with them! in innocence, in solidarity, in peace, if only they may sing their song, and not alone.

PLAYING TAG

A small band of ragged boys are playing tag or capture the
flag or hide and seek in the city park, choosing up sides and
whacking each other manfully with wooden sticks, eyes bright
as blood, falling dead among the boulder-bones and bottlecaps
and rising up to fight again;

the maple trees and the cool calm earth beneath their feet
don't get it; and the pigeons and the pedestrians don't get it
too; and the cold clay in the potter's field and the soldiers and
the garment girls churning in their graves don't get it, nor the
handsome cabby with the fifty dollar fare;

all this falling and rising, all this choosing up of sides, this
faux madness and dangerous noise and imaginary campaigns,
dead furious and bright;

all this playing at it and they play hard and winning and losing
and dying in each others' arms;

all this being brave about it and breathless; and laughing
about it and shrugging it all off;

death, death, death; squabbling about everything and agreeing
on nothing;

and being joyful or vindictive or worn out; embracing each oth-
er at dusk and heading off home to mothers and suppers and
unworried sleep;

all night long, the boots and blood of war march on, in places
farther off than ever a small band of ragged boys playing tag or
capture the flag or hide and seek in a city park will ever see

all night long, the blowing wind blows
all night long, the falling leaves fall

HER LINE OF VISION PRAGMATIC AND GREEN

A western girl in a western town, absent of miracles, impulsive, her manner frank, her line of sight straight as a clothes line on a windy day, a western girl and I met her in a diner and offered her my hand; and her hand pressed into mine like a seed potato into fertile soil, like a carpenter's drill; and she walked with me, and the way she laughed, plain, barely literate, but beautiful in its simplicity;

and her eyes, rugged as a miner digging thru anthracite coal, like a civil engineer, digging iron ore or phosphate or thru sweet mountain passes;

and her eyes, leveling everything off, drifting on a ribbon of highway to parts further west, her eyes already well-oiled wagon wheels, always ready to roll, two pioneers wagon-training it west, and she invited me along;

this then is melancholy, to sleepwalk with the brave;

the way she danced across the muddy street at dusk when it rained, the way she kissed me on the mouth like clothes pins, in my heat and confusion, cheerful in a cheerless town, it made me feel hopeless and hopeful and alive;

a western woman, woman of a western town, town of hoofprints and rain barrels and wilderness men, town of practical men in bowler hats and praying under church steeples and too stubborn to evade the law;

but most all her eyes, ever mindful, surveying the way west punishing the mountains for what we otherwise call love

A VILLAGE CALLED SMALL HARBOR

Village of three bridges, each a century old, village of flat stones and trout in the shallows, village of sparrows that dart like bombardiers and marsh hawks that measure the surface of the river and calculate where to swoop and where to plunge;

fly-by village on the old post road with a stone church and a leper's stone and a stained glass window inspired by Picasso or Marc Chagall;

and a nest of hunting birds that prowl the harbor where the river extinguishes itself like fire in the sea, and a moss-brown horse paddock and hayfields, and a general store;

and old women who cannot keep regrets to themselves and have to lay them on somebody or else perish; and a few old men outside the swinging door who handroll cigarettes and take their time and brag about the past;

and fish nets hardly worth mending and anyhow there is no one left to mend them properly;

trust no living soul to tell it, trust no dying poet to sing it, trust no gray bearded musician with Cossack boots striding over rooftops with a green violin to break stride and make miracle of it;

trust only the bewildered ghosts who walk at midnight and suffer gallantly and suffer it without incident;

nearer my god to thee kind of village, plow left out in the pouring rain kind of village, fisheye for everyone including the preacher and his wife;

village of cemetery plots and plain resentment and barely the will to outlive the grave;
village buried so long under the barnacle sky it has forgotten the sun, where the boats that put out to sea at 3 am return after dark;

and a young man with a roving eye could get himself caught up in a current or the mist and get himself turned around and never return.

CONTROL YOURSELF, THEY SAID, BUT I COULD NOT

Control yourself, they said, but I could not; there are other urges I obey; the wind that swings the lantern; the rain that shakes the sawgrass; the great stone that grinds corn down by the bushel, where the river falls;

control yourself, they said, but I could not, for there are other urges I obey; the truth unstrung, that disguises itself as legend and shears the heart like a scything knife; the wound un-healed, that disguises itself as law and lives many lifetimes and makes a mockery of youth;

the primal fire, that burns like an unholy kiss and has no name except fire; and lightning, lightning, which strikes and strikes the willow, and lights the darkness surrounding you and me;

(and the grinding stone shall crush the corn and make liquor of grain; and the river shall declare itself in the newborn's cry; and the wind shall resurrect itself in the widower's eye and express itself in love's new caresses);

control yourself, they said, but I could not, there are other urg-es I obey;

the cowbell in the mowing field, the soul in its shallow grave that plucks the lyre; the revolutionary herald that waits just below the surface and prepares to burst forth and ring anew, like a sweet storm in spring;

and the shepherd with his flock, who knows much and says little, and holds his tongue 'til shearing time, like a shy child in primary school who finally raises his hand in triumph, having known the answer all along.

BUFFALO SEED

Let's drive west to dangerous Los Angeles make love among
the huckleberries lasso the sun dive face first into the wind
like sharptail grouse two Geiger Counter heroes shapeshifters
mad navigators crawling naked across the canyon floor eat-
ing seagull sandwiches pitching puptents scattering shrapnel
in Mormon territory surfing the undertow sleeping on park
benches with crazy Jack London;

let us cover ourselves in suckervines and duckblinds and howl
and howl! lower the boom scatter the dew let us go off road let
us dance like shaggy monks on shimmering sands legendary
high on peyote groan like seacreatures shout terrible haiku
into the mystic;

let us tow the junkie out of the ditch and swing enormous jack-
hammers;

undo our belts in the rain hold court like coyote when the
moon rises let's drive west let's get dangerous let us experi-
ment with rattlesnake fate and play the deity defy the past two
resurrection engineers gold miners fossil hunters lumberjacks
tweak the nose of old man Trask and the cabbage king mock
the uranium hunters in their grandpa dungarees;

let us waste our nights with pig iron dreams let us ride the lone
skiff into the mist prowl the deep-dark mackerel chasing night

as we go
light hearted
wind-tossed
and free as
American
buffalo seed

WAITING FOR THE FALL TO COME

Hard left at old intolerance junction, October rising cold, here
in the late modern era we ascend once more to the heights, vil-
lains of the old-fashioned, black and white dichotomy, haunted
and isolated and shamed;

to the very pinnacle we ascend, heirs to the chivalrous cha-
rade, glorified and mortified by the code, dancing a mortal
tango, debased, fallen;

heirs to the dubious excesses of the orthodoxy, perfect saints;
heirs to the penitentiary and those who elude it; a man saddled
with his own appetites, a woman saddled to the appetites of
men; habitants to the chapel shadow;

I see shadows everywhere; rummaging in the ruins, pulling at
trunks and caskets and trousseaux, an inheritance of shad-
ows, birds rising as if to escape from themselves;

I watch from brick wall and high window, already fallen; and in
the long gallery of unearned pride and the taste of iron and stiff
collars, I study the portraits; and know brambles in my mouth,
and the stirrup and the whip;

and it is almost November, there will be ice and rain soon, or
worse;

and we will be no wiser to our own ways, even as the plains
and prairies rise up and consume us, though the winesap offer
temporary respite; and the blackberries all go back to their
maker, the blackberry god; and the children of our children to
another god, more barbaric, already yellowed with age;

even the bees will abandon their stations, the spiders their
prey; though in the stables the smell of horseflesh will linger,
and semen and blood; and in the capitals of men, the incur-
able stench of injustice, and the iniquity of false promises, all
cinched up in the dogma, a sense of inevitability;

and the horses, the horses—the horses, who bridled high, and
trampled irrationally and well—where shall they ride? and the
nations, mighty and sterling and restless and flawed;

and all the beautiful women and men, masters of wealth, in their glory and pretense and presumption and doom, where shall they dwell?

THE OLD DAYS ARE OVER THE NEW DAY'S COME

Excuse me now but tell me father are the old damaged days
finally over has the new day come – come on daddy tell me
true is it Christmas Eve again with sugarflop and sweet lip of
human kindness? is it the night to dress the way we used to
dress and laugh around the hearth while a toy train toots from
station to station and power strips power every family tree?

O plug it in
O come on daddy
O let it be forgiveness finally let it be you and me, her and him,
let us step up to the plate and shoo the old mistakes out of the
stable
O let's get a damn drop on our terrible selves and start all over
again a drop of mercy in your eye it couldn't hurt;
O a cinnamon stick in every man's cup
O let us spike our brains with Christmas tattoos;

cut us a break, appledunk our hearts; let us go shoulder to
shoulder with the big kahuna and cookie cutter gingerbread
man; sandbag the foolybear of unreasonable joy; prance the
snowman, fix us shapeshift us pixie us offer us diamonds from
dust, light our snowbound way;

O maestro offer us your Christmas belly your good cheer and a
sweet bowl of bottomless hope;

would you would you would you would you bid us peaceful
night; would you would you would you would you send our
way the good blow of your innocent smoke;

would you would you would you would you deliver unto us our
better reflection our lost cousins and unforgiven sisters and
brothers and twinkle the hall with wrapping paper;
unload the overcoats! sit down together and raise a chin high
toot of loose champagne!

O Christmas you have got us on our knees; deliver us back to
the immaculate star!

now let the salt run freely back to the sea
now let the crustacean shrug off his sorry shell
now let the prince of Christmas butterflies reign
now let the dwarf of peace from every dark cocoon emerge

WHEN MIDNIGHT COMES

When midnight comes I will lift a cup in a crowded room be-
cause it is New Years Eve and that means new hope and the
delicious amnesia of smoke and mirrors of wine and witty for-
getfulness;

I will lift a cup to rounded shoulders and worn out hair and
empty my eyes and plant my feet firmly on god's good and
familiar and disappointed earth, and for a couple of hours not
feel the ground shake or bear witness to the graves desecrated
or the vineyards robbed;

I will allow my attention to drift from face to face in search of a
friend or lover I never once let down or who never let me down
and anyhow let bygones be bygones and put aside all that has
been half-forgotten;

I will lift a cup and find some rhythm or musical phrase or
detail in the dead-ass room, some sign of life to sway my dy-
ing soul, some promise in the vaudeville and the malingering,
put aside the politics and restlessness and fresh inhumanities,
rediscover the one urge the world is not yet hip to and never
will be until it is probably too late, old as the world and not yet
exhausted or wasted;

I will go through rooms of strangers and laugh and sweat and
curse, I will share the same slogans and the same jokes, I will
swap the same tears and insincere kisses, I will shrug off the
usual errors and cheap shots and celebrate the extraordinary
and the delusional;

I will sing a last new song, put aside the inventory of miscalcu-
lation and heartbreak; I will stop for one hour the counting of
human cost and casualties; I will go through rooms and rooms
I no longer wish to travel in and never much inhabited anyhow
except in pursuit of unfulfilled desire, and welcome in the new
year and set off fireworks and dance;

and attend to my underground dreams, and lift another cup
to my lips; and celebrate the bitter fruits of the working man's
love and labor, and be glad.

DESHABILLEMENT

I do not mind the green parrot with the freakish beak the size
of a Latin American tyrant who follows foot traffic all day long
with a look of fresh menace and eager predation and resides
in the first floor window (beside a Tri-colour flag which waves
endlessly from a cast iron railing across the way);

But I must object to the immodest matron who lives side by
side with the bird and displays utter disregard for the finer arts
of deshabillement (several patrons of the 3-star Hotel Claude
Bernard have noted the same and gone so far as to accuse the
woman of flaunting it);

all of this has been mentioned to the authorities and recorded
in the travel brochures and online hotel ratings (not to mention
brought up myself on six separate occasions with the decidedly
indifferent concierge)

PERRIER

What more bitter luxury
   on the banks of the
     Seine than to be
   an old man with
    an empty heart
& a full cup of coffee
   distracted by
    a woman
   with eyes like
    two black stallions
   drinking Perrier
& reading Pierre de
   Ronsard's Les Amours
de Cassandre

JEANNE HÉBUTERNE IN A YELLOW SWEATER

Jeanne Hébuterne sat
in a yellow sweater
a yellow bird
without a cage
on the painter's edge of unreality
uncommonly beautiful
uncommonly still
uncommonly
married to
Amedeo Modigliani
who refused
to paint in her eyes
(O the prison bars of the male gaze)
she wasn't the
only one
(O how I wish to color in those eyes)
if only to see her
tubercular husband
as she saw him,
coughing by the nightstand,
if only to see the
narrowness of Paris,
viewed from
her family's fifth floor
apartment window,
if only to measure
the distance
between that window
& the cobblestones below
(O the emptying out of desire)
Jeanne Hébuterne
in a yellow sweater
Jeanne Hébuterne
in an elongated stare
Jeanne Hébuterne
in a strait-back chair—
gentle, shy,
delicate, equivocal,
Jeanne Hébuterne,
heavy with child
the very semblance of all that was

considered beautiful
to the man with
the paint
all that was
considered worthy
of being
captured (no,
read that
embalmed)
(no, scratch that,
immortalized)
in the elongated days of Paris
after the war

Jeanne Hébuterne
an easel wife
innocent as light
a brushstroke away
from suicide

MY ROSE OF DAMASCUS

She had a recipe
  for pain
    that knew
no boundaries
  an appetite
      for larceny
  a taste for
French poetry
      a pocket knife
  to puncture
      bourgeois expectations

she was possessed
  by parlor light
    and dark angels
she had
  a list
    of lovers
        long as a
peacock feather
    she wore
  marigold attar
    and cashmere

her intimacies
  were maddening
    her affairs
theatrical
  and her lips
      to me
  were copper penny
boulevards
  her voice
      was rain on cobblestones
    and I,

    I was infatuated
with her hands

ANTONIN ARTAUD IN A STRAIGHT BACK CHAIR

At the foot of
his bed in the
Hospital D'Ivry
sur-Seine (in the
suburbs of
Paris) sits
Antonin
Artaud in
a straight back
chair he is
not sleeping
he is not crazy
he is having visions
he is enacting
a ceremony
of pain
he learned
in the last
furious orgy
of peyote vision
he experienced
in Mexico—
exorcising demons—
the nurse folds back
his crisp white
sheets—
no use!
why do they even
keep me here
when there is
nothing at all
wrong with me—
just a little opium
for the artiste—
    he demands it of visitors
        he demands it of the warden
    he demands it of the gardener
who looks in on him nearly every day
and understands what the others cannot
    what is this fresh cruelty!?
he shakes his head

he shakes his fists
he shakes his walking stick
of knotted oak—
this cane belonged
to Jesus he shouts, it belonged
to Saint Patrick, to Lucifer!
let me out of this hell
I must go to Ireland
and return it!
no use—
is it his fault
he is possessed
of occult faculties
he learned in the land
of the Tarahumara?
in the hallway light
all night long nurses
pass back and forth
like jungle cats

they never look in on the great Antonin Artaud;
he will show them all who they are dealing with!
the gates of paradise will
open at his command—

Thus Spake Antonin Artaud!
like a hurricane in palm fronds
like ferocious applause
like a sea of
red poppies
breaking
against
white
stucco
walls

THE LADY AND THE UNICORN

In tapestry no. 6
        the Lion
with his massive paw
        and wagging tongue
    and the Unicorn
        proud and prancing
                casually aroused
    are basically unaware
        there's a lady
in the picture
    or that it is she
        whom they serve;
    neither the Rabbit
            in his patch of green
        nor the Songbird
    shitting in his
        dumbstruck tree;
    only the Monkey
        in the dim lit geometry
    of the Moyen Age
        knows
whose bliss it is
            commands this scene;
        only the monkey
    in his chafing collar
and iron chains.

FEMME RECHERCHÉ

Even in the
estimable
present I
remember
you in your
early days,
seated in
the plaza
Saint-Michel
at half eight,
alone in
a crowd,
waiting for
your latest
suitor to
arrive (there
was a simple
geometry
in your
manner,
pearls
swung
generously
at your neck)
the waiter
chattering
endlessly
around us,
like a little
bird hoping
to catch a
crumb (au
table a circle
of admirers,
inside the
cafe, Delibes'
flower song—
a pedal point
held to the bass
while the voices
of two sopranos
flirt above it),

Paris was eternal,
young and tragic,
Paris was a dying swan
in the arc of the sun,
held fast to the breast,
& you with your
perfect wrists
and your
terrible
French (how
the Parisians
objectified you)
   & I was not yet ready to let go of love
(I was a
minor figure
in your orbit
the one who
knew you in
Chicago when
you were a
schoolgirl,
so what?)
how you
deceived
them all!
you w/ your
natural
grace
in the
artificial
light of the
Latin Quarter
(all bustle &
ambuscade)
too perfect
to be true, too
human (the
musical arc
Pythagoras
dreamed
aloud)
as day
drew down

ALLONS VOIR SI LA ROSE

It has rained
12 times
On the
Five
Bridges
Of Ile St
Louis (aka
Ile de Vache)
Where
    Parisian
Cattle
Used to
    Graze
& Washer
Women
In their
Slippery
White
Smocks
Grappled
With the
    Under
  Garments of
    French Aristocrats
    Until there
Was no
    Future in it
  Since break of day
Twelve times
It has rained
    & the scent
  Of rose water
    Permeates the
Morning air
  Five
Bridges
Lead us
To the heart
  Of Ile St Louis
& the children
Who cross

Over them
    Sing Allons
Si La Rose
    By Pierre
de Ronsard
    Clear
As cow
Bells
In an
Alpine
Field

It is a
    Tradition

THE SCISSORS OR THE SWORD

In the Mero-
    vingian period
the 6th arrondissement
    was prone
to flooding,
    beyond that
lay open
    meadows
dry enough
    to build a church on
this one aka
    the eternal resting place
of Childebert I, aka first king of Paris
whose consolidation
of the realms
was the choice
between murder
    and submission
aka
'the scissors or the sword'
whereas in 1926
Boulevard St Germain des Pres
dry enough (the rain
    little more than
a soft mist,
as Hemingway described it,
      resting
          on his hat
and in his untroubled
      young
    American
beard)

RACLETTE

Not far from the little
    alleyway where Lola
the Red bit the nose of a
    riot policeman during
        the 68 student rebellion lies
the old fondue joint
est 1902 not too busy
    for this time of year
so the gypsy waiter
    takes his sweet time
mounting 21 steps

carrying a dish of
    German fingerling
potatoes
and a demi wheel of
      Alpine cheese
to an attractive family of three

      seated under the grinning skull
of a particularly dead Swiss boar

SNOW IN PARIS

sometimes the Queen of Sheba asks the wrong question
As if God created men and angels for his own enjoyment;
as if God created men to share the beatific vision;

as if all these centuries we have been asking ourselves the
wrong question;
as if all along we knew that everything depended upon snow
falling on the Boulevard St Germain at night;

as if there was something peaceful in snow, something redemp-
tive, something blissful and rare;
as if the face of god beams back at us from the river as the riv-
er rushes openly past;

as if the eyes of the homeless might open and the mouths of
the poor might be filled with neon light;
as if there was something to be understood beyond the news of
the world, something to be tested, beyond the cleverness and
study of wise men;

as if there was something that exists which is answerable only
to the beasts of the field, and the wings of birds as they cut
through air;

Reason beyond reason, light beyond light;

it began with snow on St Germain des Prés, and Paris knew a
grace beyond its usual offering of grief and joy; a light in the
darkness, an enunciation, an unspoken answer to a riddle not
asked;

it began with snow, like golden roses, like blessings from the
hands of the old pope in Avignon to the wicked, and broken
and the damned;

and all the demons, spectres and spirits in the empire couldn't
stop him.

I AM STONE

I am stone, the religion of stone, its mate and its government,
I am walls of Avignon, Oscar Wilde's prison, I have been paid
for with broken bone and shackled neck; I am grappling hook;
firm as the grip of an emperor on his empire, not precious or
rare;

I am stone, I am an oath, a levy, a moat, a spell;

I am the workers standing shoulder to shoulder against the
bourgeoisie - I hold my place and bide my time!

Build of me a temple, or a bridge to cross the Seine, or a pier
for a bowline;

I am the stone at the leper's window, the cobblestone, the curb
solicitor at the door of royalty; heave me at tyrants, hold me up
against the sea; hoof or heel me, I remain, I endure;

I am catholic, saddled, barrel-busting, I am a channel for blood
and beer;

Sling me at bible goliaths – let me work
Secret, penitent, solitary in the masons' hand—
Perhaps I am in your hand now, angry;

Or cool as a lovers' embrace
    engraved by Camille Claudel
by the light of a new mad
Mediterranean moon

TERRIBLY ALONE, ETERNALLY YOUNG

Sainte-Beuve was talking about Millevoye the poet, who loved
to write about death, not life—elegies to the young, glamorous-
ly written, romantic and doomed, 'woods that I love, farewell!',
when he wrote 'There is in most men a poet who dies young,
while the man lives on'

Whereas Vincent, just 22, had fifteen more glorious years of
poetry, paint, and hell ahead of him, when he became pos-
sessed of Sainte-Beauve's fine approximation, madness, not
one for whom life's primal dream was likely to vanish into
humdrum work or the business of life

22 or 37 or a hundred, a man in whom the poet will not die is
young forever, not even a revolver shot to the heart can kill the
poet inside a man like that – the man dies, the poet lives on –

DATE 27 July 1890, nearly dusk
LOCATION in the village of Auvers-sur-Oise

Vincent Van Gogh—absorbed in an immense plain with wheat
fields boundless as the ocean, delicate yellow, delicate soft
green—left his easel against a haystack for a moment, went
behind the wall of a nearby château, and fired a bullet into his
chest

Mad to live, mad to die, young and alone
terribly alone, forever young

LE FEUX MAL COUVERT

The baker's boy with
flour in his hair works
    seventeen hours a day and has
no time for romance.
    But he cannot hide
the love he feels for the
flower shop girl on Rue de Montreuil.

"My love for you is fresh as
    new baked bread," he declares,
attempting to be poetic.

Though he cannot find an appropriate rhyme, he means every
ounce of it.

Her heart leaps like a lamb in spring –
    though she is experienced in poetry
she is completely inexperienced with boys.

For the moment their love
burns bright. The flower shop girl
    has read Racine and knows
a flame that's poorly covered
    burns the more bright.
        For the moment
they are inseparable.

She has lilac in her eyes, He is bold as rising dough. Their love
is doomed.

After all, a flower shop girl
on Rue de Montreuil
    who has read Racine
cannot long resist a boy with
flour in his hair

who cannot find an appropriate rhyme for bread.

THE LAST BACCHANALE IN THE MOLL DES PESCADORS

Hardly anyone recalls the name of the pretty ballerina from Kiev, with eyes black as mussel shells and legs like knotted bread, she had bad teeth and modernist ambitions, fell head over heels in love with our little Pablo and was never the same, they had to resuscitate her with open palms and a dull kitchen knife;

Hardly anyone remembers Eulalia of Barcelona, the young virgin exposed naked and whipped in a public square for openly professing her faith during the age of Diocletian, a miraculous snowfall in mid-spring covered her nudity, a celestial admonishment to civil authority, they hid her body from the Moors a hundred years and finally buried her in alabaster;

And who shall write of the modernist glory; and who will rock sweet Gertrude in her cradle?

Pablo played the Catalan flute on a Barcelona rooftop for his good friend Carlos, but then he beat it for Paris.

Outside the cerveceria the six-month bride from LA, star of her own movie and pregnant as a river, has walked off with three slim cats from Bohemia, wearing zootsuits and toothpicks ties; they were très très, they were looking for whores but would settle for less;

The fourth cat stood motionless beside Gaudi's tomb in the Basilica and Expiatory Church, motionless except for his lips, he prayed like a highwayman in a rainstorm, he wore a 15th century apotropaic amulet around his neck and was protected by the armament of Christ the Man of Sorrows;

Hardly anyone plays the flabiol y tambori on the rooftops of Barcelona anymore; death, plague, tourism and other everyday unexplained misfortunes rule the city;

The cobblestones of Moll des Pescadors ring hollow, pigeons foul Gaudi's magic fountain;

But a little crowd is always gathering, it is always gathering, at a quarter past one; and Catalan hearts will always beat faster than pistons in the gasoline night;

And if ever there is a crash, and God in his heavenly glory fail to forbid it, may white doves fly from the people's mouths like gasping angels.

YOU WANT TO TOUCH SOMETHING, SO YOU TOUCH IT

You begin the way you always begin, you with your own very
precious story; a psychologist a socialist a pothead and a priest
are playing golf and it starts to rain; so they stand under a
shelter and kiss and kiss and kiss and kiss, until one of them
gives birth to you,

everything you talk about begins with something else, but ends
up being about you.

first you wanted to kiss me, give birth to me, then you wanted
to suffocate and subdue and destroy me.

in your world such things as these are possible:
a gorilla gives birth to crocodiles,
a crocodile gives birth to tadpoles,
a tadpole gives birth to a leather handbag carrying your birth
certificate, a packet of goldfish, some lottery tickets and a sui-
cide note;

that's how you begin things, you want the story to end just like
it begins.
you want to touch something, so you touch it.
you want to have something, so you take it.

GIRL AT THE TRACK, NOT YET A WOMAN

Girl at the track, not yet a woman, honest as the west is wide, betrays her experience with a flick of her hair, knows the wrong sort of men and plenty of them;

Santa Anita girl, not yet 17, making players out of old codgers in their old codger clothes, making horses' asses out of restless hipsters, and many a well tonsured man regrets how she passes;

all eyes are on her and she knows it, though in the mist of her own mind's eye she is perfectly invisible; all eyes are on her, this child of a navy man, granddaughter of the golden west, eyes bright as brush fire on the fresh side of the freeway;

a powerful rhythm to her hips and shoulders which resembles the finest breeding and a natural equine energy; shoes by Gucci and a blue and white strapless dress; bristles like a horse that knows turf from paddock and glories in its full stride;

tall, and straight as a new torn blade of grass played between two thumbs by a dirt farmer on a plain old farm road (her grandfather, who told her if she lives to be 100 she will always look 16); if she lives to be 100 she will remain a cathedral on the edge of the western sea for men to worship in;

and she will lock them out of her own heart until the day she dies;

and her gaze will remain wide as the San Gabriel mountains, where mountain lions prowl in January; even as our gamblers' eyes remain fixed and narrow, as she ambles past;

even as our gambler's eyes search for the place where childhood ends and eternity begins; in fact the dark gone edge of eternity, where mortality collapses gracefully into the arms of the sea.

WAIST DEEP STEADY AS SHE GOES

Emerging from
the soiled light
of practical
day putting the
freeway behind
him he fingers
the pulse he
measures
the horizon
he steps into
the surf
barefooted
    checking
  this thing
out (he likes
to check
things out)
he is
still
a rational man
not yet a
creature of
    wild ride
  and undertow
the ocean is
magnificent
the shape of
his body is
unfamiliar
    all the noises
  and distractions
are yet within him
gravity counts
    he is
ankle deep he is
  not yet free
he is a
  logical man
a man of
property
the idea of
dignity, being

used
exploited,
all okay
       even knee
     deep even
stripped
     down to the
          minimum
     he is nobody's
fool he
does not
know desire
only this
          hellacious hunch
        that there is
something
necessary
out there
to meet
head on
     he does not
          yet get it
     he has
          not yet been
     lifted out of
his own shit
     by the Savage
          Grace of the
               ocean god
o! whiplash
     and hammerlock
the chemistry of it
     is yet out
          of reach;
wading into
the surf like
a surgeon
calm in the spill
and tremor
          this is defiance
        this is sordid fiction
               (is
          this the best
     he can do? he

        is about to
find out)—
waist deep
steady as
she goes
he mounts it
he turns into it
he rides it
like a bull
        like a
    shattering
        shapeshiftnig
    shooting
star he is all
commotion
and he turns
again and now
    it is
        coming on fast
so! this is
    lift off
so! this is
    soul horizon
"I am the god who made me!"
    he shouts
"these are my
arms my ribs
this is my brain
    catapulting
        into the halo
    of circumstance!
the big bang's
got nothing
on me!"
    he is
moonwalking
    he is all
glide and
compensation
    he is
clean—
there is no more
sin in this—
        to be alive!

yes the original
sin was birth
　　wash the blood
　　away wash it away—
this crush
these bones
this body
burst from
the barrel
he is everything
he is holy
his promise to return
to the Master
fulfilled
　he is
original
　he is
naked
　he is
gleam
and golden
sparkle
　　a man
　at last
only a man
who
has done
nothing
wrong
in this world
　a man a man
　a cannonball
　a grapeshot
his own
impulses
exposed:
　　redeemed!
　with the
spume and fury
　of the deity
which spawned
　him

IN THE SWEET VIOLENT HOUR

When rattlesnakes
  slumber
in the coastal sage
  and green sap
      in every palm tree
  loses its mind
and the madness of
  bougainvillea
     follows
  a rich woman
all the way
         down
Wilshire Blvd.
to her doorstep;
  the sweet
violent hour
when
  at the sound
of her
  footfall
that divine
  young animal
her
  lover
emerges from
the
  shadow of a
eucalyptus grove

WOMAN OF MINE WOMAN I HAVE NEVER KNOWN

Woman of mine woman I have never known, you are as smooth as you are brown-eyed, you are sad as a setting sun (other times sugarbright as a magnet); I carry your image closer to my breast than a bounty hunter or a missionary with his cross of gold (I cross myself in black and white); and if canyons laugh and echo my pain I also laugh;

and if it makes mountain goats uneasy I will tell them your name anyway (and search many lifetimes for you); for you are in shadow where women hide, and in plain sight, and you are in the cantina where rough men go to avoid the anger in my eyes; this is what it means to love you, like few before me ever could,

until long after I have passed on from this place, to far greener pastures than these.

MAMA BEAR IS HAVING

Mama bear
   is having
        one of those
   days in the sub-arctic thaw
of Parsippany New Jersey
   where the Martians
        landed in
   1953 her
      three cubs
         have got their
   little paws stuck
              whilst
dumpster diving for
   frozen fish sticks
      behind the daycare center
         where Mz. Destiny
      a blue-eyed marsupial
at the tender age of
         twenty-three
      does such an
   amazing job
with snacks and lunches
   for the little ones

   They are not only delicious
but healthy too

RAIN IN CANARSIE

2 train rolling gonna
get off at Newkirk-Little Haiti
head down to the
precinct house where the desk
sergeant will be shaking a couple
of quarters out of his
pants pocket not enough for coffee
gonna be a long night
he has that dark look on his face
like a vase of wilted flowers
a long night ahead a rough night
ahead on account of the rain
whatever your circumstances
whether you have got a desk job
or riding around in a patrol car
like a moving target
and messing w/blow monkies and whores
or dressed in blue smoke
cruising with the waterproof angels
avoiding your own reflection
or sitting in a parking lot like a
sarcophagus with a radar gun
and the wipers on low
rain pouring down all over God's own creation
hot as melted butter
and all that bluster of wind
and boredom and dangerous communion
it is not a pretty sight no sir
it is not a pretty sight
        a life powered by combustion engine
and the light turns red-green-red
and thru the precinct house window
you can see it's warm
and some of the boys are probably
playing poker and all the usual
small talk going on but
here's us
out here in the cold
graveyard shift
it's a long shift hard rain
falling

slantwise and straight
at the heart
like a hospital needle
and likely to go right on falling
right through to shift change
another night gone and wasted
like a ghost in the juke box
but morning will come
down at Marine Park there'll be
seagulls flying and pancakes
and waitresses at the Atlantis Diner
and all the gutters choking
and midnight faces
like black lilies
will go back to normal
and life will be
clear as Jimmy the Bag Man singing
yes morning will come
and the traffic in Canarsie
will applaud its own survival
and stride confidently
        into day
like airplane passengers do
after a dodgy landing at JFK—
that's right there'll be handshakes
and congressmen
sunshine grift and harmony
and plenty of protection money
to collect on the boardwalk

so much winning!

and all the subways in Brooklyn
will run on or close to schedule.

ON OLD GOWANUS BAY

There'll be hell to pay
  when Scrapper John, 82
    a puller of barges
  since the age of sixteen
    with his blue eyes
 and cooperative disposition
stops playing along
    and spills the beans
  on what goes down, exactly
    and for who
      not far from
    the wet berths
  and graving docks
on old Gowanus Bay

HASHISH SPIDER

What if I was eighteen again
what if a hashish spider
crawled out of the spigot
and into the hotel room
and bit me on the derriere
and crawled out of the
room so I couldn't prove
it; what if my skin didn't turn
purple and my ass didn't bubble up
and I didn't bleed from both eyeballs;
what if Carol-Ann didn't have pretty
blonde hair and her boyfriend couldn't
play guitar like Jimmy Page and hadn't
been to the desert and seen spiders
WAY bigger than this one; what if
spiders have their rights too; what if
getting outside your comfort zone
is romantic and a kind of liberation;
what if a man at a travel agency ought
not to be trusted; what if I just shut up
it was only a spider or else just a hashish
spider and never crawled out of a sink
in the first place or messed with an
eighteen-year old boy like me.

RADIO FLYER

From time to time
a landslide of grief
overwhelms the lady
who works behind the
perfume counter on Rodeo
Drive; when no one is looking
she cups her hands and buries her
face into them; she smells the
fragrance of primrose sweet
as dusk, and she gives in
to it; it's all too much, she
loses the calmness and self-
control her work requires
of her and cannot unsee
the grave they buried her
child in; or the little red radio
flyer, overturned in the street, with
its white wheels spinning

WOMAN. MAN. APPLE TREE.

Growing older has not taught much patience to the apple tree
nor wisdom to reign in the orchard,

The great trees have seen their day, yet go on bearing fruit
anyway,
stubborn as peasants wearing holy rags.

Rude as mockingbirds.

Generations of lovers pass the orchard, walking hand in hand
and laughing; the young men go confidently

To their women, and fruit comes thick to the branch; the red
fruit
thick and bruised as fists; Woman. Man. Apple tree.

To each woman her Adam, and to every man his Eve! May ev-
ery one
remember their place in Eden, make love openly in the sun,

And then lie easily together afterward, naked to the waist
beside some nameless little stream.

BURLESQUE ROSE

Passed too far from
hand to hand
no longer even sad;

 All there is
to savor about love
or mourn
has long since passed;

A soulful song
    mishandled by
          some colorless cover band,
a summer afternoon

Robbed of its heat;
no hint of grace
or fragrance
in the burlesque rose;

It is a barren thing
    aping the buoyancy
of love's first offering.

A FISHER OF ROSES

I wish peace to all my lovers, and bid the beasts
   rest easy in the muddy fields of their sacrifice

not knowing the day or manner of their execution
   not knowing I am a fisher of roses among the thorns

I have loved them all and love them yet
   all their kisses all their kindnesses

all their madnesses and hope
   their patience in disillusionment

and the taste of their breath as they rise up to greet me,
   perennial, from the soil, at day's first breaking

for they are the earth out of which the sweetest corn springs

EMPTY AS A JUG ON A WINDY HILL

Stones do not
        speak
    they listen:
wings in forests
    hooves on trails
the sowing of seed
    the amplitude of dreams;
all the sounds
  overlooked by men
    from the prison gate
from the madhouse window
    from the foot of the bed
where newlyweds sleep;
    it is the fate of man
  to miss all these;

Stones do not
speak
    they listen:
as for a man
  he may stand
    on a mountaintop
  a half a day
or a thousand years
  he will remain
    empty as
a jug
  on a windy hill;
    and never know
  what counsel
a stone keeps

  or the tortured
 sound
    of human souls
winging their way
    to and from
heaven

LOOKING FOR MAGRITTE

I would say
      seated in your kitchen
   in yellow light
         tonight
   the treachery of images
does not haunt you;
      but this is not
         a poem about
               you, or
            kitchens, or
   disillusionment;
this is a poem
         about
   the way light
         enters a room,
      any room,
         say
   a little room
 in a little library
in snow country,
      for example;
         it is first snowfall,
      actual snow
         is falling;
how quietly
   light enters the room
         from a tall window,
            looking for Magritte,
         not finding him,
      settling instead
on a blue woman
      scated at a
         blue table,
            her hair pinned back,
rereading Mallarme;
         she is a pipe
      that cannot be smoked;
         her shoulders are blue
      as oysters,
blue as smoke;
      her heart is beating slower
            than clocks
         among all those books

URBAN HEART

Urban heart wattle and clay
fingernail held to the edge of the sky
mortar and stone glass and steel
all weather Babylonian pothole prayer
be my golden heart hang by a thread
be my quick on the trigger, quicker
in two way traffic, urban heart,
terrible at detail good for
one refill; buy me a ticket
make me happen;
early withdrawal
easy off ramp
one stop rubber heart,
surprise me, drug me,
make me easy for mugging,
double bag me against burglars;
keep me cool under pressure
double glaze me, keep my eyes
to the ground; urban heart,
cool me in your ice cream cone;

Urban heart springboard city
transient and empty and gray,
short dive me into a concrete pool
where the pavement meets the sky;
engineer me, handle me,
give me wings, wind shear me
board me up in icy weather
lock me in your subterranean vault,
parade me in spring where the bums
and butterflies and mermaids go;
spray me on tenement walls after midnight
by the light of the yaya tree;
swallow your pride spit yourself out
clean yourself up laugh on cue cut in line;

be innocent
be beautiful
be omnipotent
be conditional
and blue;

tear love down build love up all over again.

HALVED AND HALVED AGAIN

I savor the customs of my people, as you savor yours, hammered over coal and ember, resilient, laughing proud in the wind, egoless in the face of temptation or predation;

no prey to invading army, no cowering under cover of night, vagabond and free, stirrup to heel and worn to the bone, sustained by strong hand and common seed; no prey to rank or purchase, immune to seduction, respectful of self and modeled in modest appetite, molded to oarlock and trim of sail;

I sing the customs of my people as you do yours, and the wages thereof, stirred with a wooden spoon, visionary, firstborn, specific, and cover my body in spring with twig and woven flowers, cover it in winter with animal pelt, wedded to the earth;

I ladle from a cast iron pot, I pass it around and smoke the communal pipe when night comes calling; I sing my people, and you sing yours, in new crop as in old, no compromise no bowing down except to sow or reap, under a benevolent sun, and in accordance with practices handed down by the gods and partitioned at the gates of Eden, cast out into the earth, separated from each other, made manifest across the earth by dispersal and differentiation; halved and halved again;

from soil and water I come, from soil and water you come also, equal, well born and sent out into the world by hoof and by wheel, by wind and by wing, elemental, radiant, immutable, various, all-abiding, and sacrosanct; given to us each our allotment in heritage and prayer; let us listen to each other, with respect, and learn;

this is what makes us whole; this is what give us solace; this is what makes peace possible between us.

WORDS

These orphan words
  which follow me home,
    these poor few words
      dressed in rags,
        brushed aside
      by others,
   I set traps for them
  with my heart
as bait;

  I take them in
    I sit with them
      by the fire;
        they can fool around
      in the kitchen,
    they can hang from
  the chandelier
for all I care;

for they are marvelous to me;

and when midnight comes
  I let them out
    and dream by the fire
      of their many adventures
    and accomplishments;
  and I am blue and calm
    and at peace with the world

    because they always
  return to me, always!
    in the morning

    with their tails
      between their legs
    their confidence
  restored
  their innocence
intact

AND NOTHING SHALL STOP THE SEA FROM RISING

Not the ripple nor the reel, not the dancer nor the chef, nor
hook nor juggler nor sodomite nor thief, nor reef nor chariot
nor charioteer nor pharoah drowning in his last ounce of impe-
rial pride;

nor the ant-eater with his tongue like a gluestick, snuffling up
his last earthly meal of termites and ants;

no nothing shall stop the sea from rising, not the mystic nor
the seer, nor the shepherd nor the fool, nor the businessman
in his blue suit of business best, nor the honeybee nor the hye-
na, nor lizard nor homegrown garden wizard in his overalls and
widower grief;

nothing shall stop the earth from shaking nor the sky from
breaking out in tears;

nor sand crab nor sacrificial lamb, nor Hollywood producer
and his crew of expensive cameramen, nor the tone-deaf waiter
standing at the five star table
with his teeth bared
like a friendly crocodile;

no nothing! not even the priest who threatens everyone within
slashing range with his sacrificial knife;

the sea will rise and sweep past cop cars and mountaintops,
past dinnerbells and Miranda Rights, will shoulder through
cities ignoring red lights like a small fry gangster on his way to
a meeting with the big boss;

the sea will rise, and nothing will stop it from taking payment
due, nor plankton nor plankton eater, nor empty nester nor po-
litico, neither the mendacious nor the wise shall hold sway, nor
the tv repairman nor the jungle king on his coconut throne;

only the small fish, who will gather sweetly, green and lumi-
nous, at the bottom of the sea;

the small fish, who will gather and keep close to each other at
the seabed, and wait;

the small fish, who get shouldered and shouldered and shoul-
dered aside in every tide;
they will look up from the bottom of the sea and look up, as
they always do, helpless and godless and without wonder or
dispensation or mirth

and survive.

12 POEMS IN TRANSLATION BY ROBERT DESNOS

THE 18 METER LONG ANT/LA FOURMI
An 18-meter long ant with a hat on its head?
　　That doesn't exist.
　　　That doesn't exist!

An ant pulling a cart full of penguins and duck?
　　That doesn't exist.
　　　That doesn't exist!

An ant speaking French, and Latin and Javanese?
　　That doesn't exist.
　　　That doesn't exist!

And why not?

THE GARDENIA/LE GARDENIA
Once there was a gardenia.in a garden in England.
An old lord appropriated it, to flower his buttonhole.
.　　Since then, there are no more gardenias in the garden.
Nope, no more gardenias.

THE LILAC/LE SERINGA
Let us beat a tom-tom to Seringapatem! Let the trumpet sound.
Today is the day of the party.

Lilacs and rutabagas! Hail to the lilacs! Shame on the rutaba-
gas.
　*Seringapatem is the name of a fortress in Mysore, India,
where English forces sieged and defeated the armies of Sher-e-
Mysore, the Tiger of Mysore.*

THE LEOPARD/LE LEOPARD
If you go into the jungle, beware the leopard who meows under
his breath and comes out of nowhere.

In the evening, when he purrs, a nightingale will sing cheerful-
ly, and the yawning jungle will listen and be surprised.

Very surprised, really, that right there in its woods there lives
a leopard who meows under his breath and comes out of no-
where.

FOUR O'CLOCK/BELLE-DE-NUIT

When I go to sleep and begin to dream, La belle-de-nuit gets
up. She enters into the house by climbing the balcony.
  A ray of moonlight
  follows behind her,
Belle-de-nuit, midnight flower.

AT FIVE AM/A CINQ HEURES

At five o'clock in the morning, in a new and empty street, I hear
the sound of a car driving away.
  An alarm bell begins to shout like broken ice.
  Shattered glass shines in the creek.
On the pavement there is a pool of blood and a little smoke
dissolves into the air.
  Ahoy! Ahoy! Tell me what happened.
  Wake up! I want to know what happened.

Tell me about the adventures of men.

THE PELICAN/LE PELICAN

Captain Jonathan, being eighteen years of age,
caught a pelican one day on an island in the Far East.
In the morning, the pelican laid an all-white egg,
and out came a pelican bearing a striking resemblance
to Captain Jonathan.

  The second pelican laid an all-white egg, from which inevi-
tably emerged another pelican who did the same.

This poem could go on for a very long time
If you don't make an omelette.

THE ANTEATER/LE TAMANOIR

Have you seen the anteater? Blue sky, grey sky, white sky,
black sky.
Have you seen the anteater? Blue eye, grey eye, white eye,
black eye.
Have you seen the anteater? Blue wine, grey wine, white wine,
black wine.
    Nope! I didn't see the anteater.

He has returned to his mansion, and there, with his long

nose, he has snuffed out all the candlesticks.
Now it's all dark.

TO LANGUAGE, THAT PIT VIPER
You're killing me. So obedient! But I'll die one day anyhow. I'll
know this ideal woman, and I'll snow into her mouth. Slow-
ly. And I'll probably rain into it too. Even if it's late, even if the
weather's nice. And I'll let fall a tear too. Without reason, of
course. And without any sadness.
We love our eyes so little.
So damn little.

TO THAT LITTLE DAY/AU PETIT JOUR
Will shale light up the sleepless night of the cork? Will we lose
ourselves in the midnight corridor with the calm horror of dy-
ing sobs?
Hurry up, all you famous lizards, climbing plants, carni-
vores, foxgloves, famous since antiquity!
Run through the vines! Whistle up a revolution.
Run giraffes, I invite you to a great feast!
The light from champagne glasses will be like the Aurora Bore-
alis! Women's nails will strangle swans!
Not far away, there will be dry grass on the side of the
road.

LADY WHALE/LA BALEINE
Pity, pity the lady whale, who swims without losing breath, and
feeds her little ones cold milk, with no guarantees.
Yes, but they have such small appetites!

Pity, pity, the lady whale, who in the depths of the ocean sleeps
among seashells, under the wakes of tugboats and ocean liners
that sail on open waves.
She makes a nest there for her giant babies.

THE PIKE/LE BROCHET
The pike makes plans. I will go, I will see!
The Ganges
The Nile
The Tagus
The Tiber
And the Yangtze River.
I will go, I am free to use my time.

And the moon? Will you go see the moon?
Traveling pike? Bad-hearted pike?
Pike of good fortune?

WASHERWOMAN/LES
Washerwoman, washerwoman! Have you seen the blue fish
who was swimming in the river? He has brought you lavender.
Lavender in blue bouquet.

> Blue fish.
> Lavender flowers.
> Blue fish.

LADYBUG/LA COCCINELLE
In the Chateau at Bagatelle was born one day a ladybug who
went astray.
> She lived more than once in a rosebud at Provence.
> She was found in a thermador in a rose at Mogador.
> She avoided the sirocco in a rose at Jericho.
> She fell into a reverie in a rose at Picardy.

Lucky ladybug! Seven-spotted critter! You're a stupid thing,
but fitter than fit.

THE TORTOISE/LA TORTUE
I am a turtle, and I am beautiful. All I'm missing are wings. To
imitate the swallows. Eh? Eh?
My corset is elegant, it fits me perfectly. It requires no buttons,
or stitches. Or varnish.
I'm a turtle and I'm not wealthy.
> And I›m not hunchbacked.
> And I›m not disappointed.

> Oh really?

THE TOAD/LE CRAPAUD
There's a toad who lives on the banks of the river Marne who
cries bitterly under an acacia tree. Tell me why are you crying,
my pretty toad?
> Because it is my bad luck to be born not beautiful.
There's a toad who lives on the banks of the Seine who croaks
his breathless song in total gibberish. Tell me why are you

singing, my ugly toad?
    Because I am very beautiful.

From the banks of the Marne to the banks of the Seine I sing
my pleasant song, with the Sirens.

LA FAMILLE DUPANARD

The Dupanard family, parents and kids, live in a shack in Vitry
sur-Seine. O what luck!

Old man Dupanard made his bacon, got out of the glasshouse
and made his way to Vitry, Vitry sur-Seine. O what a windfall!

Old lady Dupanard was a mess, she sorted herself out in the
end, and drinks Pernod in Vitry Vitry sur-Seine. O what terri-
ble breath!

Young Louis Dupanard usually sleeps in a jailhouse, but he
packs his bags in Vitry, Vitry sur-Seine. O what a horror!

Young Louison Dupanard has duck feet and hair like a marmo-
set, in Vitry, Vitry sur-Seine. O what a diva!

In the medical museum there's only one Dupanard left who
hasn't made his bed, in Vitry, Vitry sur-Seine. O what a hard-
ship!

    Into the family vault they will all go, sure as fate.

That's death, that's life in Vitry, Vitry sur-Seine. O what a pile!
They'll all be forgotten. That's how it goes, in Peking, in Paris,
in Vitry, Vitry sur-Seine.

Sing it again!

ONE STEP FROM HEAVEN AND MY HEAD ABOVE THE CLOUDS

The clang of bells along the steep path is of no comfort or concern to me; neither does the tail of the long haired shaggy before me nor the low steady grunt of the yak train behind me rile my blood or trouble me or disturb my gait; I haul the long haul, I am steady on rock and mud and river crossing alike, and on the steep path below Neptse peak I take each step lovingly;

the Yarsamgumba hunter in the Annapurna, who crawls on hand and knee in search of magic mushroom, does not distract me, nor the lead yak, my brother; my master's voice is clear and pure to me as a Nepalese fiddle; I carry propane and rope, cookpot, trunk and trousseau equally; un-bemused by wedding scarf or the song of court women who produce sons for their lords and masters;

nor does the smoke of a thousand cookfires nor the summit stir my blood; coarse snow cannot blind my eye nor sway my load;

the stove burns both ways, I love my master and my master loves me; I do not scan the road for politeness or woe; I am the riprap and the hoof, one step from heaven and my head above the clouds;

you may lead me with a string; I celebrate the looming abyss and carry on.

IF YOU SAILED AWAY

I would sail away I would sail away with you; walk with blue
feet across blue oceans, fly with green wings through forests
of green, glide like yellow kestrels over yellow Canadian plains;
I would chronicle my path in fresh indigenous tongues, follow
trail of silk and thread of needle, cast dice, invent divining rods
and floating compasses; dwell in nests and learn the blueprint
of eagles;

I would wade into white clouds where the hush-hush bird
resides; lie with the lion and land where the rainfall lands; I
would stow away in iron hulled ships and bust through every
border and boundary known to man;

If you sailed away I would gather al fresco with the women at
the stream and joke with them and learn their secret knowl-
edge; wear new shoes; hammer out the grail in foundries that
belch smoke and shit out trowels and airplane parts; master
hand riddles and rapping plates, drowse among the poets and
magic you up in eternal poppy fields;

I would work with small men whose only dream is to enlarge
their dreams; I would float like milkweed seed to where earth
secretes its greatest promises; sail in cupped hands; leap from
the earth like liana vine in a land of big cats and snakes, rattle
like plates in the cupboard of joy;

and squawk victorious in the presence of your smile, like a
great rooster in the holy mountains of hope that greets the sun
and is glad for the break of day.

DAGGER OF DAWN

I am the poet of gravediggers and elusive women, my boots trample through Eden's gate, poet of icon-busters and drunk soldiers my heart is my weapon the swamp is my home; I breed in mud with the larvae and give birth to narcissus flowers;

I am the ointment and the cure I open up wounds and pour elixir in, I revive the dead I tear innocents out of the unworthy womb and nurse them into being as if they were children of my own;

milk comes out of my breast prolifically, I fulfil unrealizable dreams;

I am the hoof that carves the mountaintop, the miscreated, the paragraph that just goes on and on; the poet of inhospitable places, I swing in empty playgrounds I make men weep in the rain; I am the unintended liaison, intoxication itself, my body is my own and really, that is sufficient and enough;

I am myth and meter, poet of storm clouds, friend to wild stallions and untamed lovers, and young; I return life to the uninhabitable regions and spread lavishly, opulent as a carpet of desert flowers;

and my tongue is sweet, sweet! as the dagger of dawn over ruined cities.

TO BE LOVERS, PURPOSELESS AS TROPICAL RAIN

A prisoner is in his cell, jungle country and it is a hot night in August, stifling really. first scent of a hurricane barreling in from the east and the coast has already opened its arms to its lover, the sea.

even a jungle cat needs air, as much as a prisoner lying on a cot in a cell needs air.
okay it is the authorities who have dumped him here. he could have kept his head down, he could have kept his mouth shut. but society is simply too much sometimes. we all know that.

sometimes society eats at the heart of a man, gnaws at his bones. sometimes it is better to be locked up inside, where a man can do less damage to himself and to others.

outside if a man isn't careful he could beat his head against the walls that surround him so hard he bloodies his skull and crucifies his brain. inside he can better survive a society that has already bled him down.

in this, he is a beautiful animal, wild and unconventional. untamed and untamable. admirable really in his delicate exile. particularly to one prison guard, who hates his job, and takes little satisfaction in believing that justice is about the redistribution of pain.

o his eyes! says the guard to anyone who will listen. pale as orchid petals. o his arms, strong as the branches of a kapok tree, father of all animals. he admires the prisoner so bad it hurts him to his soul.

this is no conventional story of lover and loved, abuser and abused. it's just two people fated to be this one unusual thing together, this one unnamable thing, their lovemaking consensual and furious and helpless. and sad, in its own fashion.

they are in a season of their own, two lovers, purposeless as tropical rain.

late at night you can hear them lying together, the low moan of their breath voluptuous in each other's mouths. their soft cries audible through prison walls.

even outside the prison, where society ends and the jungle be-
gins, you can sometimes hear them, and their hearts pounding
fast.

fast as wild animals, and their caresses stronger than the on-
rushing tide.

flesh against flesh, cresting in the night. sacrificial as all hell
against one another's breast.

ONE SUMMER EVENING DEEP IN SERIOUS PLAY

One summer evening deep in serious play, with all earth clad in brimming green, and ducks in the duckpond and cattle in the stall, I walked out into the sun, clothed in human consequence, to see what I could see;

dust rising so slowly on the old north road even the hounds affected no interest; and rainclouds stalking the western perimeter;

overhead the world was crowned in yellow and blue, a lone hawk circling beyond my sight and back again; woe to the field mouse, woe to the garter snake; and the candor of farm machinery rattling fields of tobacco and distant corn;

I walked out into crops, orchards, fallow lands; past stables, past lace curtains and past yellow lamplight and fat little oven-bellies stuffed with pie;

and the farmhands at table, with their hard work pride and their no bullshit musk of sweat; insolent, laconic, putting their furrowed hands together in genuine prayer;

all the residuals, all the intents, all the aspirations, put aside; yet the scent of the untamed in every nostril, indomitable;

even the broke down bunkhouse mule could smell it; even the lumbering possum could smell it; and the axe-handler, hip deep in kindling wood; and the farm boy, stream-wading with fishhooks and backward glances, looking to upset one last beaver dam or ruin a songbird's nest;

all among us, denizen of weed, denizen of swamp, denizen of wasteland and the wasted, displaced tenants and wandering sullen priests of the wild, could smell it;

summer at its grandest height, summer at the summit, not yet giving way to fall; all that is good and golden and green, on the verge of going under.

there is no malice to it, nothing to confess;

I walked out into the sun, to see what I could see; and rose with the river rising; and lingered with the sun, long-lurking on the floodplains and beyond black cottonwood trees.

HUNGER

To slander to scheme to roll the dice; to crave recklessness;
to dance on the edge of reason; to make an orphanage of your
father's dreams;

to eclipse the void with marriage sex or quadraphonic equip-
ment; to hatch to hate; to build a hermitage of pain in a whis-
key bottle;

there are some men who use money to hide the fact that they
are reptiles;

there is a hunger which makes one man sing and another man
blunder hatless in the furious rain;

to crawl to fly to fling ourselves madly into the arms of any
woman or man; to hoard to spend to murder to cure;

to empty the pockets of our fellow man or to fill our pockets up
with quicksand and stones; to dodge existential dread; to sepa-
rate ourselves from our self with impetuous desire;

there is a hunger that makes one man guard his heart and
another man stand fast in battle and trust in god and not shit
himself;

one man whispers another man moans one man meditates an-
other man slumbers beside a sweet flowing stream;

one man manufactures weapons of war; one man catapults
himself into a ravine; one man drives himself to the madhouse
in a pink Cadillac; one man crosses the finish line dead last,
but he crosses it;

and one man holds a newborn in his hands,
welcomes it into a world he does not understand
yet must command or know the reason why.

AN APRIL MORNING HALF SO GOOD AS LOVE

O for an April morning half so good as a trenchcoat on the first
of May when the new sun, slinging ludicrous and free with its
paleolithic mud-luscious manner, promises daylight to trees
and germination to grasses; and the sweet carpet of forest
flowers bluebells the hillside and day grown longer than in the
cave-mouth of winter gaping;
an April morning half so true as the corrosive laughter of crows
that mock men in March, fading in winter shroud, and the long
forward view toward summer and blackbirds returning to the
fields and springwater offering its breast and breath to the tru-
ly loving and truly loved, the one song sung freely;

O do not ask who deserves euphoria such as this, an April
morning half so good as me loving you and you loving me back,
and a mist of riotous cloud dissolving skyward like a swarm
cloud of bees seeking sun - honey - heaven, and the inexorable
warm horizon and the good news everywhere;

yes an April morning immutable unalterable and half so true,
half so good as love, which proves itself and prospers without
trying; love holding counsel with itself all over the stunned and
miraculous countryside, the one song blowing gray and green
and gray again; like gods and hearts and the first lucid flowers
of spring;

love doing its unaccountable disagreeable best to fuck things
up, and beautifully.

A FREEDOM FIGHTER'S SONG

They displayed his body in the copper mines, they displayed
his body in the laundry houses; they displayed his body in the
slaughter pens and shit-house walls; in prison dining halls and
ghetto windows and at the steps of the factory gate;

they displayed his body to frighten the children of the poor; the
children of the innocent, the alienated and the disenchanted
and the damned;

they hung him out to dry; they strapped his body to a mule
and hung his body on a door: they printed his picture on the
front page of a big city magazine; and they whispered into the
ear of the grieving, in their grief stricken bed, and into rice
bowls and geranium pots; and into the mouth of the widow
praying at the bed of her orphaned children;

we have killed him! we have killed him!

they marched in victory parades, they hung banners in the
branches of cherry trees; they displayed his body naked as a
hillside, naked as a light bulb, naked as a virgin child, riddled
and bullied, humble as a side of beef on a butcher's rack;

but they could not kill him, they could not kill him; because
he was wide as a continent and confident as the wind; even in
death, with bullets and poetry bleeding out of his body, and his
love of freedom to sustain him; and the sweat from his patient,
working man's hands bled sweet;

and the people whispered, he is alive, he is still alive! because
the people are stubborn, stubborn as mud and straw, stub-
born as an accusation that spreads through the countryside,
smeared in blood on the side of cantinas and courthouse walls;

because the people keep the truth alive and their heads togeth-
er, beneath deafening skies; because poetry is bread, and pro-
test is the providence of the people, and must be shared freely;

because warplanes can streak victorious across the face of
heaven all day long but they cannot cast shadows that will
overwhelm the vision or purposes of a determined people;

because he was their victory and their voice and their child;

they snatched his image from the dirty hands of the murderes,
they took his words out of the mouths of warlords and propa-
gandists, they fed his body into their own mouths and restored
his image and gave his incorruptible name back to the soil
beneath their feet;

because he was as soil to them;
their soil, no one else's;
live as seed, strong as freedom,
precious as souls on the wing

THESE WORDS

These words move like mist on a hazardous shore, are oblivious to everyone; these words are divine, and delicate in the mouth; shy, self-evident and always playful, they sway with subway cars and hover like hawks over canyons of deep shadow and sun;
these words hide in a great cedar forest, guarded by gates of complex gold; gather force in desolate places and descend on cultivated plains by hoof and chariot, and are righteous to a fault, and furious;

and when their fury is spent, they are helpless lost boys who miss their mothers and peer through cottage windows and admire what they see inside, pillowcases and soup spoons and kitchen fires;

these words are golden mist of unreality, they form up like an army that passes through eternity, they are crawling with insects and have wings to fly; they live in the ravings and justifications of teenagers and the beautiful incredibly naive;

therefore this poem is a meadow, it is sensuous, and senseless, and ripe; it leaps like dolphins, it is fruitful and lingers like the scent of plums on a sailor's tongue; it drinks from a scripture of waterfalls and spends twilight in working men's bars with actual metalworkers coal miners, actual teamster union men, actual thieves on parole; and takes orgiastic pleasure in holding outlaws to its breast;

what strange intellect has brought these words here? I haven't a clue;

these words dance their private dance and do not explain themselves to me; they sustain songbirds; they bond like alchemy they are like the hearts of deer cannot be divided; they have blessings to offer, warnings and admonitions; t h eyes have sweetness of disposition;

they come from the provinces, these words, and return to them unscathed; they pass their days peaceably beyond orchards and hold commerce with asses outcasts and honeybees; they dwell in sadness and in milk, and in the eyes of women are ghost-like, unapproachable;

these words are cunning, they keep low to the ground and give nothing away, except love, love, and longing for love; and are always handy to hide a hare, fill a sail, or craft a quick get-away;

no myth, no mystery, no gods to hold up or men to hold down; these words spark heavenward as if from a Mycenean signal fire;

therefore this poem is a grail, therefore this poem is a portent, therefore this poem is a DNA footprint on a volcanic lost pre-historic shore;

therefore this poem is innervoices and accidental awakenings; it is wings spread out on a raw windy mountaintop

MA JEUNESSE

I take your body I take your hands I take your youth in the
cradle of my arms, and offer you my love; blue as the blue sky,
yellow as the immaculate sunlight, careless as a planet making
its first rotation through heaven;

Ma jeunesse! your hair your mouth your little fingers, your
smooth body, innocent as silk; your steady gaze and infant
odor; you are perfect, we are perfect, your mother loves you,
your father loves you; you have a dry bottom and a belly full of
milk;

I stand here at the nursery window, curtains parted and the
darkness all around us, and raise you up like an opera, like
a masque, like an orphanage of pain; and I ask it of the gods
from which you came—why are you crying like a jaybird in my
arms?

AT ANY MOMENT ALL OF THIS COULD DISAPPEAR

At any moment all of this could disappear, someone could come into this room and rub things out; your womanhood, my childlike point of view, my bleak and bizarre devotion to un-fashionable fictions;

at any moment, at any moment, all the pots and pans of my honorable co-existence with reality rattling in the dark, the hall light flickering with horror or self-doubt; love, intention, re-spectability, sucked from the room, all this could disappear;

at any moment, the dull ache in the belly resembling desire; at any moment, the emptiness that accompanies too much fu-ture and not enough now; at any moment the hole in my heart which will not close;

I am an amulet, I am a figurine, I am Loki the shape-shifter, dancing on the eyelids of sleep; I am a minotaur, a semi-pre-cious stone; I am a fading rose in a faded dream;

at any moment, all of this could disappear, and be replaced by a promised land beyond the American guilt-consciousness;

sunlight pouring in from the western horizon, red brick roof-tops and a stitchery of leaves;

a flutter of wings, a cage with no bird;

bourbon on ice, poured freely by hand, with a hint of Miles Da-vis to level things out.

THE HOLY GOOF

In the beginning there was peace on earth, men and women were free, and life was full of promises and time; then came god, and things got thick and dangerous: god gave mankind tribes, and miracles, and war;

and things were pretty good until the soldiers came with iron swords and iron armor and iron chariots; so god gave his people slingshots, ox-goads, and the jawbone of an ass, and 700 left-handed men to sling right-handed stones at the soldiers;

and he bid them fight, tribe vs tribe, and win, and lose, and fight some more;

and there was no more peace on earth, only history; and the miracles ran out.

so god cut off the end of some men's penises and sent them down into Egypt as slaves. 'this will make a nation out of you,' said god. 'you will be blessed among peoples. and cursed;'

call it a covenant. call it a test. call it a con or a compromise. call it a holy goof. I don't know what to call it;

god's purposes on earth are mysterious.

IN THE ABSENCE OF MIRACLES

In the absence of miracles I made this little song to wander around the city awhile, wander at a safe distance from broomsticks and door handles, to perch in awnings and billboards and disobey traffic signs and discover everything is small and wonderful and true;

a little song to follow young lovers from corner to corner and crisscross fashionable boulevards and trip on cobblestones and shine like neon shines, intimate and charming and bright;

a little song to sit in the uninhibited cafe and dream like wise old libraries and saunter on the riverside or race across the big lawn with its great green grass and sunlight spreading everywhere on modest little wings;

in the absence of miracles I have made this song, warm as milk and true as jazz on a spring afternoon and the seabirds calling down by the harbor and everything safe pretty and fine;

and the city hall cops and the little mayor on his soap box can't stop me; and the referees of good sense can't stop me; a little song for the baker closing up shop after a four am start a little song for the barber on his feet all day a little song for the barkeep just climbing out of bed and rubbing his eyes;

I made this song for the five o'clock whistle and the six o'clock train, for the passersby passing by; and the cherry trees pink and roundly blossoming; and the pretty young girls breaking promises and the pretty young men rubbing shoulders and laughing naturally and secretly wishing they were John Reed or Jack London or Ernest Hemingway;

for the lonely blue pigeon waiting beside the little green bench hoping some humankind will come along and feed him a few little crusts of bread;

and the daily news and the laying on of landlord hands can't stop me; and the rude canticle of glass and concrete can't stop me;

a simple little song to play along with, to co-exist with; a simple little song to sing together or alone;

a simple little song to make miracles of its own;

and the great gray imperfect barrelhouse piano key cityscape sky, overhead, chiming in.

FAITH

The subject could have been anything, really; the price of eggs,
salt and cucumbers on a countertop; anything at all, instead of
the subject that ailed him;

battles fought and lost in domestic war,
      the hydraulic scent of engine parts
         cranking through hostile clouds;

and she would have loved him for it, and wanted to make him
whole again; beyond the color of his hair, mustard flower in
sunlit Dijon fields; beyond the rattle and bone of his voice, a
goat track through the Pyrenees;

beyond the cold brightness of death in his eyes, burst of can-
nonfire after the fall of Bilbao; the way he held her face in his
hands; the wordless way he let her take him in;

because she gave him calm, like the presence of god in godless
places; because she gave him purpose, like the possibility of
honor in a dishonorable land; because she gave him fierceness,
beyond scripture of love, beyond textbook of devotion;

the kind of fierceness required to drive past cemeteries in cold
light of day;

the kind of fierceness required to sail a scuttled coracle home
through green sinister Aegean waves.

TALL AS CACTUS IN CROOKED DAWN

Nevada will blossom yes the whole Great Basin will blossom, we will dance like opera house boys in the downpour we will break bread with strangers cradle the dead lay bare our breasts and lie down with our enemy;

it'll be knife to the barrelhead, whiskey to the glass;

and we will dance mad as bottle rockets with our fists in our pockets and glass in our veins, and the desert will flower all around us like glimmerships and small creatures drawing new hieroglyphics and spanning continents;

pass it along, pass it along! ancestors to our own mortality, eaters of eternal ash and mystic vision, meandering awkward as stick bugs, inheritors of the hitching-rail, orphans to our own alleyways roosters to our own kind;

imminent as spit and bundles, buriers of hatchets, our hands conjoined our bodies raw and chapped, meek before gods; four masted, particulates in the tall cloud, one with the core of our radioactive ambition;

O what quintessence! O what paragon!

slave by slave carrying the basket shouldering the load milking the sagebrush fed on succulents a nourishment of wind blood flesh and bone, casting long tawny shadows across sky country;

saddled up tall as cactus in looking-glass dawn, one with the gray-haired ghost who lives down the adobe road and reigns supreme in western mountains.

LIKE A PRISONER IN A SPANISH TOWER

Like a prisoner in a Spanish tower, like a widow at the widow's jar, like a pauper at a poor man's grave, I am bound to you, I walk with you, in blindness, irretrievable; and you hold me fast, like a junkie at the well, like an innocent drunk on too much wine, like an ambitious man foundering in a sea of self-mockery;

like a mystic at the gates of hell, like a village in smoldering ashes in volcano country; like a novice at the doors of the speed casino, sick with demons and begging for more;

I walk with you and would be yours, and have you penetrate me; and pierce my feet and hands with wellsprings of underground water; I would have you clothe me in nakedness and unclothe me, mend this life I have lived too fast, and unwisely;

unstain the deep tattoo of my callousness, release me into the storm of your fierce, voltaic caresses;

and I will do this and that for you, and I will declare new allegiance to old truths, be they half or whole, and the unblemished heart; though I am barefisted and ridiculous; though I am bleached to the bone, though I am ruined by the long cast of false appearances;

I will beat the very sky with raven wings, furious as the last hopeful stroke of sunlight to quiver a leaf;

terrible as the eye of a jungle cat stalking the perimeter of a world gone mad is terrible;

made fearless, made wise.

DRUNK ON THE MAD PROSECUTION OF LOVE

In a land of pure eternity and time to waste, love was easy so I wasted my time with you, on a rooftop, in a dorm room, in an Amsterdam cafe; once upon a time in a movie that still plays in my head where you ran hot and cold, cooked me in a spoon, gave me handcuffs and roses, freed me like prison breaks and shovels full of dirty money;

once upon a time, three thousand miles from everywhere;

once upon a time there was you and there was me in an impossibly orchestrated predetermined nest for two, high in Malibu, hunkered down in K-town, unorthodox in Japan, Zen as homespun cotton, very hip, very casual, a sweet decantation of inexpensive rice wine; and who needs the stars when the radio's playing and there are miles you can count on along a lonely stretch of Baja desert road;

once upon a time you walked me in and out of love, once upon a time you turned me off and on like sunlight after rain, once upon a time Las Vegas and Chaka Khan could not illuminate a world so bright; and the clock on the mantel nodded its head and counted down the hours, like a silk rose on a countertop, our little smokebomb of love going tick tock tick;

and we went from doom to doom, in a stairwell, in steerage, in a bluebird hotel, under dwarf palmettos by the light of a southern moon; on the wing with all the crickets chiming, drunk on the mad prosecution of love you demanded (and what does a boy of twenty-three know about love)

YARA BLANCA

They call her Yara Blanca
on account of the white cape she wears
in summer or in snow
she lives in the land of work
like the rest of us and does her time
honorably, like you or me
she does her level best
to be indistinguishable
from the crowd
in bars
in beds
in hillside grottos
    burning with shame
        and desire
in chambers of
solemn quietude
she lies in waiting
in hidden places
comes out after dark
and can find her way home
in total darkness
Yara Blanca! she is
a tiny butterfly
dressed in white
apart from the crowd
which has its own work to do
while all the little white butterflies of the world
go on searching for themselves
and each other in the crowd

A TINTU CUMBIA

Three in the morning, sky a kind of
Tintu Black
the high cordillera shrugs its
muddy shoulders and blinks out loud
to see so much joy and unrestrained
car honking in the crooked streets
and boulevards of Medellin –
life is disorderly and good - a strange
and confident little shakedown
has taken over this town again,
with its sad eyes and beautiful women
No More Weeping!
    the end of days is also a beginning
for the wicked and the pure
it is three am
    it is the poets
they are holed up at the Gran Hotel
    they are dancing

BLINDED BY THE PRESENCE OF GOD

Day by day, hour by hour, it occurs to me; a birdhouse, a mail-box, a Rolls Royce in a parking lot; a lion in a cage, the Jersey Meadowlands flooding at quarter to ten; day by day, hour by hour; a kid of 16 hustles for quarters in a poolhall; a neighbor-hood girl, thin as a straw, makes wishes on a dandelion head;

day by day, hour by hour; this carnival of hope, and pity; an old man snoring in a new spring breeze; a wet blanket tossed on a blue chaise lounge; a little worm crawling thru acres of bristling corn; a large careful woman in a widebrim hat; a pick-ax stuck in a bed of clay; a red wheelbarrow covered with fresh mud and several years' handsweat and rust;

malice among friends; envy tossed like rice at a wedding veil; appleblossoms falling from an appleblossom tree;

all these things amuse me equally, damn my eyes; I am blinded by the presence of god

THERE IS A CITY WITHIN A CITY

There is a city within a city that feeds on the abyss within, writes manifestos concerning the oblivion of self, lapdances on tenement ceilings, drummed reggae on gleaming tile of public urinals; a city of omens, a 2 a.m. city, a skidding celebration of get-away tires and the sharp report of gunfire outside a 24/7 chicken joint;

there is a city inside a city, a city of street level busts and secrets spilled safely in the company of strangers; a city that refuses to justify itself or its occupations, wholesome or illicit or impure; a rainbow cloud of a city, that welcomes muggers, drunks and stoners of all stripes; a city of roommates quarreling through paper thin walls; a temperamental back-sliding city of broken pavement, easy love affairs, high heel shoes;

there is a city of first-time sinners and long-time losers, a city that never looks down and never looks away, a closet dreaming city, city of users and the used, of single men on the prowl, and armies of furious women patrolling dance floors on hot humid nights that melt the senses;

a city within a city, that sheds its light in dark hours of thermonuclear despair, suffers abandonment, embarrassment, hope extinguished; a tender city, tolerant of precipitous failures and small miraculous victories in sad cafes; a zero-gravity city, a city of promises fulfilled; a rank and file city that throws itself to the mercy of the pavement from rooftops and climbs back to heaven again, undeterred;

a city that executes forbidden tangos, climaxes in a public park, pisses in full view of the authorities and laughs;

a city bigger than itself, and more majestic than the plague.

I HAVE SEEN HOW MADNESS WINS

I have seen how madness wins, burns bright in the eyes of beasts and men freed by the song of the siren or a faint beacon of light set out on a cliffside by shore pirates;

I have seen freedom from the lash take hold in the imagination of horses and men, freedom from the knotted rope, freedom from the bosun's mate lying bloody as brains among the sea rocks;

seen the unfettered mariner break bad; seen a tight rein bid the horse run faster than a man may comprehend; thru city streets thru city gates and into snowstorms; stallions pulling their own weight, and nothing more;

I have seen leather reins torn from the brewer's fist, barrel staves bursting on wet cobblestones, the machinery of war left mercifully behind;

and wished to run as the carthorse runs, having stolen freedom back from the spur;

mad as a river overbursting its banks in hot open plains not ruled by men.

DISOBEDIENT

Because the stain of poverty colored my mother's good manners, and her uneasy laughter betrayed her shame in better company; because my father was an irony of vowels, deceitful as a catbird, orphaned by the American dream and proud of it, a masterful conductor of damaged men, possessed by ruthless charm, an inadvertent stealer of the hearts of women;

because my sister spoke in sweet ellipses and fooled me handily; because I had no brother to help me translate the world into ordinary English; because my other sister did not bother to address me at all and only gave me blows to the head behind my parents' back and tossed me face-first into street gravel on three separate occasions;

because I was not born rich like my neighbors and therefore despised everyone and imagined I was despised by them; because my uncle was a wandering scholar of Anatolia and loose cannon on Fifth Avenue and showered me with paintings by Degas and Chopin etudes; because the love of words was a last resort and promised to sustain me, and so I drank a dark cup of tea in lonely libraries and kept my opinions to myself;

because I believed in the hard intuitive truth of fiction over the dull mechanics of reality; because I was suspicious of teachers and priests and idealized the kind of wisdom a state education can't buy; I kept every breakfast table secret close to the chest and absorbed every late night tragedy they could throw at me; and fed my heart my liver my lungs on fiction like a cancer;

I dwelled alone in the deep winter recesses of my childhood, unmoved by kid games and adult expectations, listless as a moth going from flame to inexplicable flame; I held my head erect when called upon in class and refused to answer;

I sat alone in long shadows of books, books, books, disobedient to all authority but theirs, and did not pray;

I read and reread them all—Proust, Joyce, O'Neill, James—by the hopeless fireside, lost in a sea of language, and did not understand a single word;

and was liberated thereby, in the long difficult flight from childhood into the holy penumbra of words.

THROWN INTO THIS WORLD

Thrown into this world, drinking whiskey and beer in a downtown bar in October, call me Dorian Gray, delivering myself from evil, waiting things out; call me a stranger to myself, learning all the latest phrases, disregarding my mistakes in a room full of the clueless and the absurd, near Alphabet City;

half a click from the East River which burns lustrous and cold, vast as all the sugarcane in Cuba, beyond the reach of time and Brooklyn's shipbuilding immigrant belly of gloom, thrown into this world, momentary;

I exist plainly and particularly in the temporary, and the bartender with the long sad disdainful Irish face and speech like poverty knows it; and the bartender with the long sad disdainful Irish face delivers pints of beer to me, and the hopped up co-hosts disappoint themselves, one by one, precisely, and without hesitation;

there are no distinctions, no directions, it's fight or fuck, it is a tired conversation that turns to death and the long reach of hurricanes that awaits us; thrown into this alone;

and I am weary of it;

for once let me transcend the hubbub and pinball tilt of urban ambition, and say no to the wizards of commerce; I have anyhow never much listened to their chatter, though I have suffered like Bukowski on a hemorrhoidal couch on their account; and have rocked like a ferryboat and rolled with the current on the River Styx; and joked mildly with the other human cargo;

and though I have ridden bareback with the Bodhisattva, escaping inevitable communists and the self-betrayal of ego punishment, and been thrown into this world, crossing the divide between madness and ecstasy, with Oscar Wilde, going too far with Jim Morrison, or toe to toe with Pollock in the Cedar Bar; and though I got nowhere for it and plenty fast;

now I take my time, now I wait things out, without you, now I disbelieve in you and the determinative lure of circumstance;

love me or murder me I don't care, I will lay me down to sleep
with you; I will trust beingness and time to work the moment
out;

why did I ever love you? I count me missing in action, I call me
stranger in a room full of strangers, I call me framed and fro-
zen; I call me the illusion of an idea, possibly a survivor, an old
gray philosopher in a plain black and white envelope;

to some things there is no season; though being and time de-
termine each other reciprocally I will have none of it;

on the grave of Heidegger I swear I will be free.

GIANT STEPS

And where will I go, in the career of days, when my mind
knows more of love's grand disquietude and of pavement call-
ing, and less of peace, and I lie dreamless under the mad flat
roof of night and cannot set down my labors or my loss, or turn
down the cover of sleep that shelters easier men, and find rest;

where will I go, in the wretchedness of lost causes and time's
passage, if not to you, where waves still sail and children like
me once played at commanding the tide with giant steps, and
hold forth against the sky, swimming like the great fish swam,
beyond the sea-break and green count of days that hang, like a
pauper's paradise, over all our heads;

one step from mankind, and a journeyman's
distance from the unpaid work of stars

PROTECTOR OF FOOLS

Crouched like a toad
    hiding in every bush and berry
hung on every tombstone
    hovering with mawkish wing
at every wrong turn
    and crazy intersection
the mad little god

    with tick tock eyes
        protector of fools
    who knows the seed
        from the twig, the flower
           from the stalk,
      and can resurrect
    a volcano from cold ash;

this is the main cat
    this is the dark destroyer
        who can get us through
    who can deliver us
        from the terrible fraud
    we have embarked upon
in the cave of good intentions

THINGS THAT OCCUR OUTSIDE MY WINDOW

This song for things that occur outside my window and belongs
to the western wind, by span of moth or eagle's mile; sparrow-
ship by wing or by song, rooks playing on bald mountaintops,
migrations plotted under the cottage eve, tender songs that rise
and fall and rise again, and small children listening;

this song, sung by the weak and the wild; this song of uncer-
tainty that outlasts spring, only to die in the arms of mortality,
and be reborn; especially the millwheel turning, after a long
winter unattended;

especially the motherbird, full breasted at her little nest,
guarding hatchlings and hanging on;

who sings her song in June,
    who fends off starlings and marauding jay
who watches and waits,
    against the fierce-eyed certainty of death and dawn

HOW FAR MUST A MAN FALL BEFORE HE TOUCHES THE SKY

How far must one hand reach before it exposes a lie? how hard must the ocean strike before the prison walls tumble and the innocent run free?

and seabirds return to the prison yard to proclaim in yawpish glee the triumph of the waves?

how many times must one heart break before all hearts are made whole? how many years must a harvest spoil before the ferment turns from vinegar to wine?

how far must a man fall before he touches the sky?

how many times must the truth be told before the tired and forgotten and the broke and beaten tell it? before the pillar embraces the dust?

and the priest lay down his chalice, and the conqueror frees his captured bride? and the rich man give up his craving for mastery and wealth,

and forsake his guile, for love?

ATHENA

Because she is an Aegean longship, powerful, sturdy, many-oared; because she is resolute in restless seas; because her interior beckons to me, and the lodestone of her natural history presses to my breast;

because she is a triumph of calm in a rowdy Minoan harbor town on a North African shore; more exotic than kind, unnamable, a leopard in star-gazing time; because she is subordinate to no one, a geode of piratical ambition;

because Pliny the Elder got lost in her bowels; and Darwin, with his impossible nomenclature, could not cage her; because she is unreality, neatly balanced, and her body possesses a deceptive skin of outward tranquility;

because her wholeness of demeanor masks a certain kind of chaotic charm that rampages in her blood;

because she cannot be reduced, because she exposes the charlatan in the hearts of ordinary men; because certain types of men mistake her for the feline that prowls their puny dreams, and other men mistake her for a stack of folded linen;

because her kisses are labyrinthine, her cadence lyrical, and her lips are a mineral bowl of gem-like contradictions;

because the wildness of her spirit is undiminished, and she is the Vesuvius of her own volcanic birth; because death and fertility wait for no man and stalk her inner Sahara;

because her compassion is as a brilliant oasis, and her voice is the whetstone of night that sharpens the knives of the despairing and the poor;

I shed my dullness, I shed my pride, like tears;

I approach her with my hat in my hand, and penitently; I open up my heart to her like a child at his first confessional, without truly understanding;

I hold steady to her body, like wind holds to a Mediterranean sail.

THE MOST BEAUTIFUL DELINQUENT POSSIBLE

I remember him as a child, holy as leather, an unwashed hero in the first boyish bloom of sexuality, indulgent, gratuitous, homoerotic, solemnly innocent; I remember him the way he used to be, an uncut diamond, confident as a renegade on a hillside beyond the reach of church; renunciator of the flesh, a poem writ in many languages setting fire to convention, questioning everything; in the schoolhouse, in the cafeteria, in the janitor's closet, the thick laughter of his ruffian throat, the impotence of his rage, and his sheer stubborn guts among grown men;

legendary, unpredictable, a little jumpy, free as sirens in the night, I remember him with turned up collar, before they got to him, I mean, racing like a car in the rain, nerves like the strings of an electric guitar, his uninhibited charm among strangers, the disarming way he deflected the advances of women, playful with authorities;

nothing could own him, not nobody, he was unimpressed with the carnival of rumors they call life; and contrary, he lived a life against society and did not adhere to any known human quality or drug;

he was street king in the violent drugstore of urban decay, he had no equal among us; in the broke down flesh, in the undertow of America; he got away with it, he kept his many triumphs to himself and had no need for bragging;

a child, child to us all, and when he got caught he confessed to everything and died casually in the empty arms of his oppressors, and was resurrected in our memory and in this song;

whole, unconquerable, ready to rock & roll; the most beautiful delinquent possible, impossible to contain.

LOVE IS MONEY, IT DON'T STAY THE CHANCES

Love is money, it don't stay the chances, nor remain in one
place too very long; it moves from hand to hand, a tender crea-
ture, the simplest possible calculation; it is a victimless crime
committed in no man's land, the big migration, the lie made
true, a hi-jacking of terrible cargo, the art of replacement, un-
tarnished among barbarians;

love is the great blind directive, the great escape, by time and
death rendered ageless; it is a holy sacrament in the unho-
ly forest, and shy; the forbidden torturous scent hinted at in
scriptures and arcane sutras; an underhanded movement nev-
er equaled in poetry or in practice; it is an art, an architecture;
an outrage, an alchemy, an instinct fragile as snow;

the authorities cannot confiscate it, nor the landlord hold
sway, love don't stay the chances or do the math;

love is the storm within the storm which lingers in the footpath
once the violence and chaos have passed; it is the first chemis-
try and the last, and while the slightest disturbance may thrill
or destroy it, love turns its face against the cumbersome ma-
chinery of calculating angels, and laughs;

it is money, it is money, and it moves easily, from hand to
hand; love tossed in the fountain, love exchanged in the street,
love ripping holes in the reactionary hides of men and furious
pocketbooks of unimpeachable women;

it is the sweet pond, turned slightly sour, then back to sweet
again; master of its own devices, in the simmering wheatfield,
in the meadow and passing cloud—nor feather floating in the
killing pool to betray it, nor bitterness to the tongue to dimin-
ish its power;

face it!
   swapped from hand to hand,
love is money,
   a victimless crime,
a meeting place of willing fools,
   a bed full of hopeful strangers;

the secret of fox and chickens, the wildebeest and antelope, undeceived by zookeeper or cage; it is the great zoo itself, the hidden bond between prison guard and prisoner; the force that divides heart from heart and draws them to each other and makes no excuses;

and it is always about to burst, a garden plot that gives and gives and won't stop giving;

until the cleansing fire returns from heaven and extinguishes the earthly odor of hell which surrounds us.

MAKE A VIRTUE OF SOLITUDE, A FRIEND OF RAIN

Love is strong, it is a thing of substance, it is a shapeshifter
and a partisan; love resurrects itself and lifts all boats and is
improbable; love is a pony, love is gratuitous, love is the idea
of you with me and me with you; especially in the beginning,
when we laughed a lot and together; a good life, you said, could
be cobbled from little things, there was nothing aside from that
worth worrying about;

if you have love you have everything, you said, and we were
two reasonable people in love, though very young, who knew
better than us?

we could not stand absences, but did not deign to make sense
of time, and sometimes you would go away and sometimes it
was me; and when you went away I stood at the door and mea-
sured out the boundaries and provinces of our union in the
terrible dark;

world without end, amen! I cursed the darkness that surround-
ed me, and fed on distractions and nightmares; other times we
lived in ignorance and in blissful lawlessness, and contentment
was ours; we brooked no bullshit and the shadow you cast
on me was the shadow I cast on you, love was enormous and
enough, beyond the material;

and love took on the shape of a snail shell or a waterspout, love
took on the shape of the letter Q or the spine of a book; and
love was ravenous, and parted its lips like snow spiraling in
still black waters;

and lotus flowers grow in dark places, and love grows in plac-
es where bodies have spilled into each other; like peaches into
sunsets and cornfields into granaries, and youth and hopeful-
ness into apathy;

and shadows are ghosts and ghosts are real, and sometimes
two hearts begin to disagree; and then they are armies met on
an unequal field, and the mistrustful and the wounded pile up;
and the emptiness in the darkness reaches deep into itself and
grows in power and ferocity;

I no longer know what happened between us; but you are not here, in shadow or in light, and I am not without tears; and emptiness is the shape of you;

I am a thing of darkness and I love you still; but have not yet learned to make a virtue of solitude, or a friend of rain.

PRODIGAL SON

Out of the darkness came another darkness, come for all souls and all societies, and the living and the dead, and the creatures on the wing, and the creature that dwells on a crust of bread;

darkness came, choked by its own smoke; darkness ripped from the belly of the planet like fishgut or a new volcano, darkness prostrating itself, immodest, rising up, wading bodily into rush hour traffic like a desert lion among the running herds;

out of the darkness another darkness came, like the sound of fox whelp whimpering for their mothers in spring; tall as cornstalks, pathetic as crops lying unharvested, pumpkins rotting under the autumn sun;

and surreptitious and proud, and camped on the outskirts of town; among forbs, clover, foxglove and gentian, blossoming like blue Illyrian kings;

call me purslane on the run; call me salamander crawling in the sedge like an alien in the mist;

yo soy verdolaga and the rusted truck made home to by raccoons, and the town runaway shivering like punkgrass in wintergloom;

along came darkness, like war, the first crime of man over man;

along came dominion, civilizations tossed to the wind like human confetti; and all the dying, the lie of the great heroic march laid bare;

and the church door unopened, and the tenement window kicked in; and the singer mocked in the village square; and the lovesong dying on deaf ears, from gate to gate;
and the sea crest throttled, and the triumph of gunpowder and open fist over love;

and eardrums bursting and uniform pierced; and buttons torn from limb and collar, and all the bloody bayonets in body-stabbing time;

out of the darkness came another darkness, and seagulls cir-
cled the island with shameless crying, and under the skyscrap-
er the secret bunker of the billionaire was unassailable;

and fear sat on a park bench and counted out its dead coins;
and the old veteran who fed pigeons in salty dawn kept feeding
pigeons;

out of the darkness another darkness came, and the headline
writers forgot to mention it; and the Sunday papers tossed
the news aside; and work like a briefcase with a broken lock
opened its ugly mouth and yawned; and the cellphone kept
ringing;
out of the darkness came another darkness, and the black robe
of hypocritical judges descended on us, and justice hid its face
and compassion burnt like cookpots for the poor;

and the profit taker went about unmasked, and there was no
more undertaker for the undertaker;

and the darkness came, and that was that;

like the prodigal son who wanders for centuries in foreign
lands, measuring his hideous pace, taking his time;

the prodigal son, cast away as a child, only to return in full
wizardry and power, to destroy nations, to pry his filthy inheri-
tance from the dead hands of society and man.

LOVE IS A RABBIT, A WHITE RABBIT

Love is a haybarn, a moonbeam, a cellar-mouse; love is a horse
with no saddle; love is a dog with no tail; love is a milk cow
that peers out through the barn door, heedless of soldiers and
war, innocent as Anne Frank scribbling at her journal, as stub-
born, as grim;

love is a rabbit, a white rabbit, a plow, a coal chute, an eagle's
scree; sometimes love calls out to me through the icy dark-
ness, from treeless crossroads and strange continents, warns
me to watch out for the devil; love wises me up, kisses me on
the forehead, sings me lullabies; love strokes me on the cheek,
strikes heart's gold like a clock strikes break of day;

love ties me up in knots, does magic tricks; flaps like wet laun-
dry in the long breeze, sets me babbling like the mother of all
fools;

love wades in shallow water as well as in deep; it skips a beat;
it disappears down a Coney Island alleyway arm in arm with
a freak show freak; it is hardscrabble, it washes away piers;
it kisses me blind as river rock tumbling into the mouth of a
restless sea;

love is a puzzle, not a prize, like treasure from trash, love is a
soldier in exile sitting idle in a foreign cafe, singing old forgot-
ten partisan songs nobody understands; love treads on solid
ground and on thin ice; it is a disappointment to its neighbors;

love carries me in its belly like a tenth month child, dreamless,
beyond all reason; or, having missed its gestational hour, car-
ries the wounded draped in its arms out of a burning forest;

love makes philosophy out of everyday simple hearts, all of
them beating steadily except mine;

love stumbles home after midnight through starless skies,
drunk on celestial languages; is a young woman focused in-
ward on her unborn child, is an old man dressed in rags and
proud of it;

love can be resolute, love can be fearless; or disobedient among the hounds; love may sound the alarm, calls all hands on deck;

love survives, love survives; on a sinking ship, at the pinnacle of pride;

love is the remains of day, and my heart gives way to love no matter how it comes.

THE SEA IS A RIVER, YOU CANNOT CROSS THE SAME BEACH TWICE

I grew up on this beach, I ran like a deer
I danced on sand and leaped from pier to pier
arms akimbo and giving voice to my youth
in the marvelous din and sweet brouhaha
and outran summer and was patient in winter
and knew no danger and knew no fear;

and the waves to me were very casual and friendly
and made no impression on me in stillness or in storm
except perhaps a percussive sound to my ear, that's all
like sparks from a bonfire, or a neighborhood dog
barking deep into the night and everyone else sleeping
and the wind curled naturally to my stride;

and the horizon rose easily to my eye
and I knew the freedom of deer, and paid no heed
to river or man, and did not know why the tide
runs in so deliberate, so wary, so very careful and slow—
like a young girl returning to a beach full of strangers
combing the brine and mischief from her hair as she goes.

AMBITION IS AN AUTOMOBILE

Ambition sings like a cricket in a clarinet case, dances like
a plastic hula-girl on the dash, laughs like a jackhammer in
Columbus Circle, tips like a banker at a Chamber of Commerce
dinner;

it drives home drunk as an oil tanker captain on New Years
Eve;

it is little thumb prints left on countertops, it is root beer floats
sweating in the sun; it is uninflated basketballs in hall closets,
greasy overalls;

ambition is the wrong clothes at the right party, the right pol-
itics in the wrong century, the right prescription in the wrong
pharmacy, the worst possible judge in the whole damn city;

it is the wrong choice in careers or men;

it is modest and in no hurry, waits patiently for the streetlight
to change, daydreams the Yucatan at street corners in ordinary
New England towns; it is Pontiacs, Toyotas, Fords; it is not de-
pressed, it just has nothing to smile about;

ambition is an ice cream truck in a beach parking lot in the
pouring rain, engine gently humming;

American made, paid for in monthly installments, and polite to
the missus, ambition is owner operated, it sits in a swivel chair
behind a metal desk, and explains the repair bill carefully as if
to a child;

it is a ball game watched from a barstool in a cocktail lounge
off Highway 41 when the clock runs out;

it can get you from here to the Jersey Shore in no time flat on
the Fourth of July, but is more than likely to break down in the
passing lane on the long ride home.

LOVE OCCURS TO ME

Like a god in a wading stream, like a waterfall wreathed in
sunlight, the froth, the bodyheat, seeking flesh to fleshy sur-
face, madness and stranglehold of the herd;

a mass, a solemnity, a stampede, a drywind gossiping around
shank and shoulder, and immersive, immersive, the hoof-sure
creature stumbling to its knees;

what magic is this, come foaming from lip to loin;

this unreal body, what barm and sparkle, what harm, what
raw weeping, explosive and interpenetrative; a welcome home
banner, soft clucking in the original mother-tongue;

a spew of trappers' blood, frogsperm, eggwater, ice in the veins;

what is this falling freely, what is this fertility dance, these
the furious details, what is this staggering, staggering, utterly
done, only to return;

love occurs to me, as a meadowlark returning to an empty
nest, as a fox penetrating open grass, as a thick-boned crea-
ture grazing prairie flowers;

muzzle-down, like death, which comes to all men whispering;
this is how love occurs to me;

shrugging off all other appetites, save these

LOVE IS

Love is an assassin's bullet that goes astray; a dog let off its leash; it is an arrow pointing both ways at the end of a dead end street;

it is a port in flames, a flatterer's memory;

love is a flat out lie, it scuffles in the back row of the movie house; love creeps in through every window, helps itself to the silverware;

it is whiskey and macaroni salad, it is a stifled yawn on an overstuffed cushion; it is the landlord scowling at the back door, rent's come due;

love is a warm spot in a marriage bed, recently abandoned; it is a kind word passed between two strangers when it's hot and cruel and indifferent as Los Angeles outside;

It is a barnyard door, where have all the pretty young horses gone?

it is a flickering hallway light, it is a servile mutt on the living room rug that barks at nothing, and bites and bites at itself for fleas,

It is a lonely brillo pad in a rusty sink, it is a cold plate of ravioli waiting for you when you roll in drunk and half past legal, and a jug of wine with the cork still in it;

love is the exception, not the rule; it is the expiration date on a blue can of Maxwell House, it is a squirt gun, and a birthday card from your aunt with a five dollar bill in it;

it's a quick round of whoop-me- darlin' on the way home from school;

love is a pink rubber ball with your name written on it, it is that chalk white zombie you met, and randomly exchanged kisses with against a chain link fence;

it is high heel parking lot, it is spray paint; it is religion; it is hanky panky under twentieth century kitchen light;

love is a neon sign that won't quit, Marlon Brando in a torn tee; it is handsome, it is neo, love wheels two crying babies down the cereal aisle, and mom is cranky as a mule;

love is neighbors asking all the wrong questions; love is a big sister who disappears for weeks on end and turns up on the doorstep with another graffiti artist, drifter, or gas house queen for a friend;

it is a box of tampons ripped off after midnight, and the check out boy winks and looks the other way;

love is always being tested, love blind sides you at the intersec-
tion of nowhere and here, love is a rescue ambulance; or be-
ing abducted by aliens; love is a flat tire on the way to or from
work;
it is a hickey, it is a scar, it is a bird tattoo you got in an aban-
doned churchyard after midnight and forgot you got, it will
never fly away;
love is being the bigger man, love is being tender when it's too
late to be right; love is the biggest mistake in your life, third
time this week;
love is hair pin turns on the Fourth of July, it is pancake eyes;
love is envelopes with Dear John letters in them, addressed to
some unsuspecting dope, unsent, yellowing, unwise;
love is flushed down the crapper by furious dads;
love is a lock of hair snipped from the head of an appalling
bride and kept in a locket for fifty years; it is nice to touch but
a real bastard to handle, and swears in a slouch hat, late to
the train;
it bribes mothers, it disobeys restraining orders, it temporarily
shuts men up;
love is torn between two bad choices or none; born and bred in
private, under covers, and really ought to stay that way;
it's a game show host, it's unsafe at any speed, love's gasoline
poured on an open flame;
love is four runaways on a mattress made for two;
it is hunting for pennies in floorboards, it is eyelids drawn thin
as a dime; love is banging for heat on the old radiator pipe;
love lies bleeding from the mouth;
smack me, love, for luck, take my hand; love me;
love rebounds like dawn; it is a new generation of lost children,
scheming their way into and out of some very pleasant situa-
tions in hell.

BEFORE EVERYTHING IS OVER

I would like to make love to you the same way a gentleman knocks on a door that will never open for him, the same way a mirror reflects the image of an old and ruined man for all his children to see, the same way a young woman discovers in the middle of a very noisy party that she is standing there utterly alone;

I would like to make love to you like a man standing on a platform at a train station trying to catch one more look at the one woman he ever truly loved, before leaving on a long journey; like a child at a circus gazing upward at trapeze rings, like crazy lights and precarious high wires, knowing he will never climb to such heights;

like the caves of Ravenna; like a washed up prize fighter stumbling face-first into the canvas and embracing it as if it is his final friend; like a bum running after a twenty dollar bill blowing across a busy boulevard;

like ravens flying blind through an eternal city;

I would like to make love to you before the passersby pass by, before the sun falls out of the sunset, before the brown bear falls into his fabulous winter of sleep; make love to you with my forehead pressed to your naked belly, with my platelets pulsing in your veins, with my brain on fire and snowflakes falling on distant hills;

I would like to make love to you a hundred times a day, made bold by the knowledge that I will never fully understand you; your Byzantine smile and untranslatable eyes, your incomplete shoulders and rainbow lips, your urgent glances, meant for no man;

because I am doomed to live with you even when I am without you—you with your imperfect elegance, you with your empty hands; you with your perfume, your aura, your manifestation of many impossible colors;

You, with the light that leaks gem-like out of the darkness and into my world.

DRIVE

I will go driving & drive the world well; press down on the little
gas pedal like a bootheel to a cobra neck; dare green lights to
remain green & refuse to be stayed by red;

I will go driving in good or bad weather & lean like a hawk into
shear of wind; glare back at headlights, lean forward & flip off
anyone who would oppose me; smash through gridlock climb
the on ramp be on my way;

incendiary, explosive, a gazelle; shun the straight loathesome
path, crank up the engine, embrace wide-eyed innocent cities
set them aflame & prove to them how beautiful they really are;

with the eyes of madness
with the eyes of freedom
with the eyes of audacity
with the eyes of mountains
& polymorphic locomotive
textures & raw python power

I will sing the madrigal of wire spoke wheels; set my jaw com-
bustible against the snarl of industry, go steel upon steel, peer-
less under the sun;

yes I will go driving
& come face to face
with destiny, put restraint
to flight, know my savior
as I know the limits
that curb or check me;
my lover, my likeness, my comrade, my friend;

& do corners, corners, corners, blind corners, insane corners,
every dreadful corner that holds men down or makes them
fearful, colorless, hostage, or mundane;

trust in defiance, toss off restraint, drink asphalt by the gallon,
crack open the American grain like a six pack of amber mist &
drink some more.

Grateful acknowledgment to the following publications in which some of these poems appeared: *Bards Annual* (Love Is); *Brownstone Poets Anthology 2025* (Faith); *CAPS 25ᵗʰ Anniversary Anthology* (The object of my desire); *Glory Hope Foundation* (A fisher of roses); *Silkworm* (Things that occur outside my window); *Sparring with Beatnik Artists* (Ma Jeunesse, This poem is a meadow, At any moment all this could disappear); *A Too Powerful Word* (It is possible to love); *Trailer Park Quarterly* (To be lovers, purposeless as tropical rain); *Waymark 22* (Halved and halved again, This poem is no memory bird); *Writing Outside The Lines* (Hashish Spider, I live inside a chalk-drawn circle, You want to touch something, so you touch it)

George Wallace is Writer in Residence at the Walt Whitman Birthplace, first poet laureate of Suffolk County, LI NY and author of 40 books and chapbooks of poetry, published in the US, UK, Italy, Macedonia and India. A prominent figure on the NYC poetry performance scene, he travels internationally to perform, lead writing workshops, and lecture on literary topics. A former student of W.D. Snodgrass (BA, Syracuse U) and Marvin Bell (MFA, Pacific U), he teaches writing at Pace University (NYC), and has done research residencies at Harvard's Center for Hellenic Studies in Washington DC. He has worked as a Peace Corps Volunteer, health care administrator, community organizer, community journalist, active duty medical military officer and local historian. His work is collected at the Special Sections Collection, LI Studies Institute, Hofstra University. George is editor of Poetrybay.com, co-editor of *Great Weather for Media,* and editor of *Long Island Quarterly* and "Walt's Corner," a weekly poetry column in *The Long Islander,* a community newspaper founded by Walt Whitman in 1838. He is editor of the 2022 Blue Light Press Anthology *FROM THE INSIDE: NYC through the eyes of the poets who live here.*

Photo by Matthew Hupert

MORE ROADSIDE PRESS TITLES:

MORE ROADSIDE PRESS TITLES:

Bar Guide for the Seriously Deranged
Alan Catlin

Born on Good Friday
Nathan Graziano

Under Normal Conditions
Karl Koweski

The Dead and the Desperate
Dan Denton

Clown Gravy
Misti Rainwater-Lites

Walking Away
Michael D. Grover

All in a Pretty Little Row
Dan Provost

These Are the People in Your Neighbourhood
Jordan Trethewey

They Said I Wasn't College Material
Scot Young

Radio Water
Francine Witte

And Blackberries Grew Wild
Susan Mickelberry

Licorice Heart
Miles Budimir

Disposable Darlings
Todd Cirillo

MORE ROADSIDE PRESS TITLES:

Full Moon Midnight
Belinda Subraman

Innocent Postcards
John Pietaro

Cistern Latitudes
James Duncan

Another Saturday Night in Jukebox Hell
Alan Catlin

Abandoned By All Things
Karl Koweski

Ain't These Sorrows Sweet?
Lauren Scharhag

Gregory Corso: Ten Times a Poet
Edited by Leon Horton

She Throws Herself Forward to Stop the Fall
Dave Newman

We Don't Get to Write the Ending
Aleathia Drehmer

These Many Cold Winters of the Heart
Ryan Quinn Flanagan

Things You Never Knew Existed
Josh Olsen

Maze
Jennifer Juneau

Green Roses Bloom for Icarus
Hiromi Yoshida

MORE ROADSIDE PRESS TITLES:

Let the Scaffolds Fall
Shaun Rouser

Apocalypsing
Jason Anderson

Failing to Fall
James Griffin

The Things We Tell
Sara Glasser